BATTLEGROUND AMERICA

THE GREAT SIOUX UPRISING

BATTLEGROUND AMERICA GUIDES offer a unique approach to the battles and battlefields of America. Each book in the series highlights a small American battlefield—sometimes a small portion of a much larger battlefield. All of the units, important individuals, and actions of each engagement on the battlefield are described in a clear and concise narrative. Historical images and modern-day photographs tie the dramatic events of the past to today's battlefield site and highlight the importance of terrain in battle. The present-day battlefield is described in detail with suggestions for touring the site.

BATTLEGROUND AMERICA

THE GREAT SIOUX UPRISING

Rebellion on the Plains
August–September 1862

Jerry Keenan

DA CAPO PRESS
A Member of the Perseus Books Group

Da Capo Press
A Member of the Perseus Books Group

Cataloging-in-Publication data for this book is available from the Library of Congress.

ISBN 0-306-81195-2
Published by Da Capo Press
A Member of the Perseus Books Group
http://www.dacapopress.com

Da Capo Press books are available at special discounts for bulk purchases in the U.S. by corporations, institutions, and other organizations. For more information, please contact the Special Markets Department at the Perseus Books Group, 11 Cambridge Center, Cambridge, MA 02142, or call (800) 255-1514 or (617) 252-5298, or e-mail j.mccrary@perseusbooks.com.

1 2 3 4 5 6 7 8 9—05 04 03

Contents

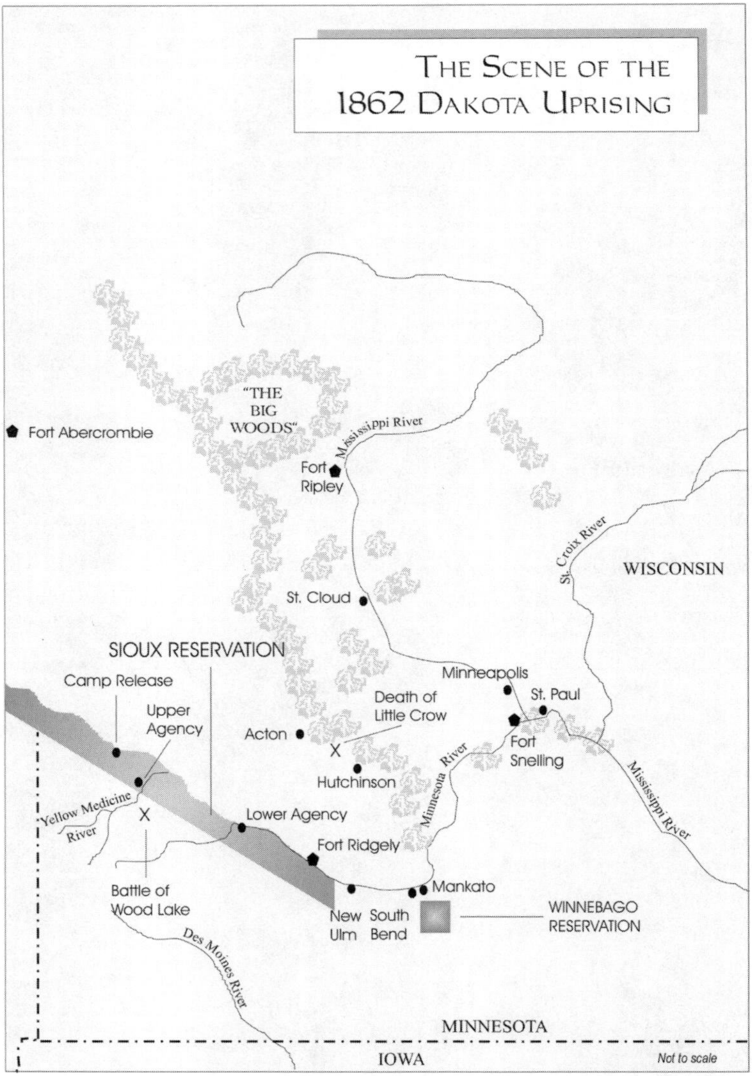
THE SCENE OF THE
1862 DAKOTA UPRISING
"THE
BIG
WOODS"
Fort Abercrombie
Mississippi River
Fort
Ripley
St. Croix River
WISCONSIN
St. Cloud
SIOUX RESERVATION
Minneapolis
Camp Release
St. Paul
Upper
Agency
Death of
Little Crow
Acton
Fort
Snelling
X
Minnesota River
Hutchinson
Yellow Medicine
River
X
Lower Agency
Mississippi River
Fort Ridgely
Mankato
Battle of
Wood Lake
New
Ulm
South
Bend
WINNEBAGO
RESERVATION
Des Moines River
MINNESOTA
IOWA
Not to scale

Theodore P. Savas

Dramatis Personae

Anderson, Captain Joseph: A seven-year resident of Minnesota in 1862, Joseph Anderson, a Mexican War veteran, commanded the cavalry known as the Cullen Guards at the Battle of Birch Coulee.

Brown, Joseph R.: Onetime agent for the Sioux, Joseph R. Brown, was replaced as agent in 1861 by Thomas J. Galbreath. As an illustration of a racially mixed marriage, Brown was married to a Sisseton woman, by whom he fathered thirteen children. He was away from home on the morning of the attack on the Upper Agency. Brown later commanded the burial party at Birch Coulee and was wounded in the fighting. Because of his familiarity with the Indians, he had the unpleasant task of later identifying the thirty-eight condemned Sioux who were hanged at Mankato in December 1862.

Brown, Mrs. Joseph R.: A Sisseton Indian woman, and the mother of thirteen mixed-blood children, Susan Brown was married to a former Indian agent, Joseph R. Brown. At the time of the attack on the Upper Agency, Susan Brown and her children, along with others, were en route to Fort Ridgely when they were confronted by a party of Sioux. Courageously standing her ground and reminding the Sioux that she herself was Indian, she and her children subsequently enjoyed the protection of Little Crow himself.

Eastlick, Merton: One of the great stories of courage to emerge from the uprising was that of Merton Eastlick. Following the massacre at Slaughter Slough, near Lake Shetek, in which his father was killed, eleven-year-old Merton and his little fifteen-month-old brother, Johnny, were separated from their mother, Lavina. Merton carried little Johnny on his back nearly fifty miles to safety at Mankato, being reunited with their mother along the way.

Flandrau, Judge Charles E.: With the possible exceptions of Governor Alexander Ramsey and Henry H. Sibley, Charles E. Flandrau was reputed to be the best-known individual in the state of Minnesota in 1862. A self-made man, he'd been to sea, then studied law in New York before arriving in Minnesota in 1853. A member of the territorial council, he was also named agent for the Sioux and later appointed to the Minnesota Supreme Court. At the time of the 1862 uprising, he commanded the volunteer force that defended New Ulm. He later accepted a colonelcy in Sibley's volunteers and participated in actions against the Indians during the remainder of the uprising.

Galbraith, Thomas J.: In 1861, Joseph R. Brown, who had served as agent to the Sioux for some time and who worked on behalf of his charges to see that they received fair treatment, was replaced by Thomas J. Galbraith, who knew little of the people whose needs he had been appointed to minister to. The timing of the change was terrible. When the hungry Sioux demanded to be fed, Galbraith refused to do so until Congress had appropriated the necessary funds. Eventually, under pressure from the military whom he had called upon for assistance, Galbraith reluctantly issued some provisions. Later, Galbraith recruited a company of volunteers to take the field against the Sioux and himself served as a member of the burial party at Birch Coulee.

Gere, Lieutenant Thomas P.: Nineteen-year-old Lieutenant Thomas P. Gere had been in the army for less than a year when he found himself in command at Fort Ridgely, following the death of Captain John Marsh in the ambush at Redwood Ferry. Not only did young Gere suddenly find himself shouldering an enormous responsibility, but he was also ill with the mumps. Fortunately, the arrival of Lieutenant Timothy Sheehan and his company of the Fifth Minnesota relieved Gere of his burden.

Hinman, the Reverend Samuel: An Episcopal missionary, Samuel Hinman was building a new church at the Lower Agency at the time of the uprising. Hinman, who numbered among his flock Little Crow and other Sioux, was one of the few who recognized the seriousness of the uprising from the outset.

Hole-in-the-Day: A Chippewa (Ojibway) chief, Hole-in-the-Day was perceived by some as another Little Crow who would lead yet a second Indian uprising. Fortunately for the white settlers in Minnesota, Hole-in-the-Day was unable to secure the backing of enough other Chippewa leaders to follow through with his plans to launch an attack.

Huggan, Nancy McClure Faribault: Nancy McClure was born at Fort Snelling in 1836, the daughter of an army officer and a Dakota woman. In 1851, at age fifteen, she married David Faribault, a trader. The union produced a daughter. By 1862 the couple was farming near the Lower Agency, taken captive by the Sioux, and held hostage until freed at Camp Release. Nancy later wrote an account of her captivity. Sometime during the 1870s, her marriage to David Faribault having dissolved, she married Charles Huggan, a farmer.

Jones, Sergeant John: A regular army sergeant and veteran artilleryman, John Jones was a holdover at Fort

Ridgely from the days when it had been an artillery post. As the one in charge of the post ordnance, Jones had trained the men of Company B, Fifth Minnesota, in the use of Fort Ridgely's several artillery pieces. It was largely owing to Jones's training that the garrison was able to use its artillery in turning back the Indian attacks of August 20 and 22.

Little Crow: Taoyateduta. The most visible and arguably the most influential of all the Sioux leaders. A Mdewakanton Sioux, Little Crow was born about 1803 and so was approximately fifty-nine at the time of the 1862 uprising. He was a signatory to the Mendota Treaty of 1851, though under protest. After the infamous 1857 Spirit Lake Massacre perpetrated by Inkpaduta, a renegade Wahpekute Sioux, Little Crow led a war party in pursuit of Inkpaduta. In 1862, Little Crow was regarded by many of the other Indian leaders as being the only one of them with sufficient influence to unite all of the various Sioux bands. He was also reputed to be an extraordinarily vain man and it has been suggested that his eventual willingness to assume the reins of command, so to speak, was born out of a need to

Little Crow

recapture some of the prestige that had slipped away from him. Before the 1862 uprising he had come to be perceived by white settlers as friendly and a Christianized Indian. Beneath the facade, however, there seethed much resentment over Indian treatment. Accordingly, when Little Crow was approached by other leaders and asked to lead the Sioux against the whites, he was at first reluctant, but eventually consented, believing the time had come for his people to seek redress for the wrongs done them.

Mankato: A Mdewakanton Sioux, Mankato, or Blue Earth, was the son of the old chief Mankato, for whom the city of Mankato, Minnesota, is named. One of the active war leaders of the Sioux during the 1862 uprising, Mankato was killed in the fighting at Wood Lake on September 23, 1862.

Marsh, Captain John S.: Marsh commanded Company B, Fifth Minnesota; also the post of Fort Ridgely. When the uprising began, Marsh led a detachment of forty-six men, plus an interpreter, upriver toward the Lower Agency. The detachment was ambushed at Redwood Ferry. Marsh himself was drowned attempting to swim the Minnesota River and all but fifteen of his command were killed.

Mazakutemani, Paul: Better known as Little Paul, Paul Mazakutemani was a member of the Upper Sioux Reservation. A fine orator, he had been trained by the Christian missionaries and used his oratorical skills to argue against the uprising. It was largely the arguments set forth by Little Paul that prevented Little Crow from persuading the Upper Agency bands not to participate in the uprising.

Müller, Mrs. Eliza: The wife of Dr. Alfred Müller, the post surgeon at Fort Ridgely, Eliza Müller and her husband were Swiss, Dr. Müller being a graduate of the University of Bern. The quiet hero of Fort Ridgely, Eliza Müller, tough, brave, and efficient, organized other women at the fort to load cartridges and tend to the wounded. During one particularly tense moment of the fort's siege, she aided Sergeant John Jones with one of the artillery pieces.

Myrick, Andrew: Perhaps the most visible single exponent of a white man with a terrible attitude toward the Indians, one who, as much as anyone, was responsible for laying the foundation for the 1862 uprising. As a trader, Myrick refused to issue credit to the Indians when they were desperate for food and other necessities. His infamous remark, "Let them eat grass," proved his own epitaph. He was killed early on by the rampaging Sioux, and his body was found with grass stuffed in his mouth.

Other Day, John: A Christianized Wahpeton Sioux, John Other Day reportedly brought back a prostitute from a bordello following a visit to Washington, D.C., in 1858. He married the woman and fathered a child by her. When the 1862 uprising broke out, Other Day remained steadfastly loyal to the whites. Before the attack on the Upper Agency, he gathered all whites in the area and took refuge in the agency's brick warehouse. The following day he led sixty-two settlers across the prairie to safety at Cedar City. Later he served as a scout for Colonel Sibley's army column. In retaliation, the Sioux burned Other Day's farm, for which the government later reimbursed him $2,500.

Pope, General John A: One of the most controversial of all Civil War generals. An 1838 graduate of West Point, Pope distinguished himself during the Mexican War. Although vain and ambitious to a fault, Pope was nevertheless a fine soldier overall. Following his questionable command performance at the Battle of Second Manassas (and the subsequent court-martial of Fitz John Porter), Pope fell out of favor with the Lincoln administration. However, after Governor Ramsey's continual pleas for federal help in suppressing the Sioux uprising, Pope was appointed to command the newly created Military Department of the Northwest. He viewed the assignment as an opportunity to restore himself to official Washington's good graces and with that in mind orchestrated the Dakota campaigns of 1863 and 1864, which ensured that Minnesota's Indian troubles were a thing of the past.

Ramsey, Governor Alexander: A thirteen-year resident of Minnesota, Alexander Ramsey had arrived as the fledgling territory's first governor. During the 1862 uprising, Ramsey was forced to try to effect a military mobilization to counter the Sioux threat, when the nation's resources were being devoted to the needs of its Civil War armies. His persistent efforts for support from President Lincoln paid dividends, however, when the president eventually appointed Major General John Pope to command the newly created Military Department of the Northwest.

Riggs, Stephen R.: A missionary to the Sioux since 1837, Stephen R. Riggs and his wife, Mary, had worked tirelessly, bringing the Christian word to the Indians. Riggs and another missionary, Thomas S. Williamson, later translated the Bible into the Dakota language. Following the uprising, Riggs, Williamson, and other clergymen argued on behalf of fair trials for Indians charged with capital crimes.

Sheehan, Lieutenant Timothy: Lieutenant Timothy Sheehan commanded Company C, Fifth Minnesota Infantry, stationed at Fort Ripley. When Indian restlessness at the Sioux agencies began to grow threatening during the early summer of 1862, Sheehan was directed to bring his company from Fort Ripley to Fort Ridgely as a backup. After defusing a tense situation at the Upper Agency in early August 1862, Sheehan began his return march to Fort Ripley, only to be recalled following the ambush and destruction of Captain John Marsh's command at Redwood Ferry. Sheehan, twenty-six years old, then assumed command of

Colonel Henry H. Sibley

Fort Ridgely and conducted the defense of that post against the two Indian attacks of August 20 and 23.

Sibley, Colonel Henry Hastings: One of the three best-known individuals in Minnesota at the time of the 1862 uprising, the other two being Governor Alexander Ramsey and Judge Charles Flandrau. Sibley, who had been in the Minnesota region since 1834, first as a member of the American Fur Company and later as a territorial delegate and first governor of the state, was well acquainted with the Indians, having had numerous dealings with them over the years.

When the Sioux uprising began in August 1862, Ramsey appointed Sibley a colonel of volunteers to lead a military column into the Minnesota River Valley to suppress the uprising. Although criticized by some for his dilatory movements, Sibley did eventually defeat the Indians at the battle of Wood Lake and secured the release of the white hostages. Later he was involved in arranging for the mass execution of thirty-eight Sioux who had been charged with murder and atrocities by a military tribunal.

In 1863, Sibley, in tandem with General Alfred Sully, led a strong military column into Dakota Territory and defeated the Indians at Big Mound and again at Stony Lake.

The city of Hastings, Minnesota, is named in honor of Henry Hastings Sibley.

Vander Horck, Captain John: A thirty-one-year-old, German-born local official from St. Paul, John Vander Horck was appointed commander of Company D, Fifth Minnesota Infantry. Vander Horck and his company of volunteers marched west across the state from Fort Snelling to take up station at Fort Abercrombie in the spring of 1862. Until the 1862 uprising began, Vander Horck and his garrison were mainly occupied in fighting off boredom and ennui. Then, in September, the Indians attacked the post, but their efforts were unsuccessful. Vander Horck was wounded in the arm by one of his own sentries. Though without military experience, Vander Horck acquitted himself well in conducting the defense of Fort Abercrombie.

Wabasha: Although Little Crow stood out as the unquestioned head of the uprising, Wabasha, a Mdewakanton leader, rivaled Little Crow as a principal leader. Like Little Crow, he had opposed the treaties of 1851 and 1858 and had signed them only with great reluctance. When the 1862 uprising began, he opposed Little Crow, though he seems to have been present at the major engagements, including Fort Ridgely, Birch Coulee, and Wood Lake. At the same time, however, he apparently organized a peace faction among the Indians and later testified before the Indian Peace Commission, pointing out the legitimate grievances endured by his people that led to the 1862 uprising.

Walker, Lucius: The Chippewa Indian agent at Crow Wing Agency, Walker, a former territorial representative, overreacted to reports of a Chippewa uprising led by Hole-in-the-Day. After calling for military assistance from Fort Ripley, Walker fled south. Apparently believing himself responsible for the Indian trouble, he eventually committed suicide.

Whipple, Henry B.: After the uprising, Henry Whipple, an Episcopal bishop, visited President Lincoln on behalf of the Sioux, pleading for Christian consideration of those charged with crimes. His argument that the white man's treatment of the Indians had been largely responsible for the uprising apparently had an effect on the president, who subsequently commuted the sentences of all but thirty-nine Sioux, one of whom later received a last-minute reprieve.

1

Background and Causes

The 1862 uprising in western Minnesota by members of the Santee or eastern branch of the Sioux nation was one of the bloodiest Indian uprisings in U.S. history, the likes of which had not been seen since early colonial times and those terror-ridden days on the Ohio River frontier. Between August 17, 1862, and the final battle at Wood Lake on September 23, there were a total of seventeen actions, including fifteen Indian attacks on the two reservation agencies, plus farms and settlements, ranging from Fort Abercrombie on the Minnesota–North Dakota border as far as New Ulm, 200 miles to the southeast. To a greater or lesser degree, the uprising touched twenty-three Minnesota counties.

In addition, the Sioux attacked two military installations and, on two different occasions, gave battle to military columns sent in pursuit of them. The exact number of settlers killed will never be known, but reasonable estimates put the number at 400 to 600. U.S. military casualties totaled about 140 killed and wounded. As always, Indian casualties are impossible to determine with accuracy, but a careful analysis suggests about 150, not including those later executed and those who succumbed while in confinement.

Like virtually every Indian-white conflict, this one had its roots in land (it was always the land), coupled with an astonishing indifference to basic human needs on the part of many traders and government officials. As well, the grim specter of greed was to be found in this late summer tragedy, which exploded like a thunderclap, even as a great internecine conflict raged elsewhere in the land.

Early traders and settlers in Minnesota found several bands of the Dakota Sioux inhabiting the western part of the new territory, which had been created in 1849. The name Dakota is a Santee word that means "friends," while the appellation "Sioux" is taken from the French, *Nadouessioux*, meaning "snake" or "snakes," which in turn was a name given the Dakota by their hereditary enemies the Ojibway (Chippewa). The Dakotas, or Santees, are themselves the eastern branch of the larger Siouan family, which includes the western-dwelling, Teton Lakota division. By the middle of the eighteenth century, the more numerous Lakotas had moved from the lakes and woodlands out onto the Great Plains, while the Dakotas remained in Minnesota and in the eastern portions of what was then the Dakota Territory.

The Treaties of Traverse des Sioux and Mendota

As settlement in the region expanded during the nineteenth century, the demand for Indian land steadily grew. The United States government responded by entering into a pair of agreements with the Indians to make more land available for settlement. Accordingly, as a result of the treaties of Traverse des Sioux and Mendota, signed in 1851, the Dakotas ceded their land in southwestern Minnesota Territory, along with significant acreage in the southeast corner. In return the Indians were to receive just over $3 million in cash and annuities, to be paid out annually over fifty years. The treaties also provided for the various Dakota bands (numbering approximately 6,000 to 7,000) to be relocated on two twenty-mile-wide reservations along both sides of the Minnesota River, between the community of New Ulm on the south and Big Stone Lake, some 140 miles to the north. The Yellow Medicine River (which joins the Minnesota River just south of present-day Granite Falls) marked a rough dividing line between the two reservations. In 1858, Minnesota became a state and the expanding settlement of the region induced the Indians to cede additional land along the north side of the Minnesota River.

The Upper Sioux Agency, which served the northern reservation, was located near the Yellow Medicine's confluence with the Minnesota River. The Upper Agency ministered to the needs of the Sisseton and Wahpeton bands of the Santee, numbering some 4,000 individuals, many of whom, however, lived in Dakota Territory outside the reservation boundaries.

The Lower Agency at Redwood (just east of present Redwood Falls and sometimes referred to as Redwood Agency) served some 2,000 to 3,000 members of the Mdewakanton and Wahpekute bands. In addition to the

Building a church in the Lower Agency near Morton

usual government buildings, both agencies included trading posts and various other buildings, though the Lower Agency was the larger complex of the two. Both agencies were administered by one agent. Agent Joseph R. Brown, who had worked tirelessly on behalf of the Indians, was replaced in 1861 by Thomas J. Galbraith, a change that would prove to have a serious impact on the deteriorating relations between Indians and whites.

The Mixed-Bloods

In addition to the whites and Indians, there was a third ethnic group, numbering between 600 and 700 mixed-bloods, or half-breeds, as they were commonly referred to in the parlance of nineteenth-century America. Representing perhaps 15 percent of the overall Indian population, these mixed-bloods were primarily descendants of Indian women and French traders or explorers, in some cases two and three generations removed.

An interesting and somewhat ambivalent group, some of these mixed-bloods had adopted the ways of the white man, had turned to farming, and appeared to have embraced the white man's Christianity. They were regular attendees at Sunday worship services. To further encourage and induce others to follow in the ways of the "farmer Indians," they received preferential treatment from the agent in return for following the white man's road. Because these mixed-bloods were well represented in and around the reservation, they played a key role in the 1862 uprising.

To understand America's treatment of native inhabitants, one first needs to try to comprehend the mind-set of mid-nineteenth-century white America, which believed in the twin doctrines of manifest destiny and Christianity. According to this philosophy, the United States of America had been ordained by the creator to tame and colonize this magnificent land. And if few Americans actually articulated or understood this concept of manifest destiny, they surely put its tenets into daily practice as the nation advanced steadily westward. Within this philosophical vision, the way to deal with Native Americans was to establish a program whereby they were absorbed into the mainstream of American society. Although by the middle of the nineteenth century, the Industrial Revolution had taken a firm hold in the United States, the country remained predominantly an agricultural nation, so it is hardly surprising that the expected acculturation of Native Americans would be through the agricultural process.

Those Indians who responded to the efforts and teachings of the missionaries and traders who moved among them were scornfully called "farmer Indians" by those who refused to abandon the traditional lifestyle, while those who spurned the white man's overtures were known as "blanket Indians," after the affectation of wrapping oneself in a blanket.

In its most fundamental sense, the 1862 Minnesota uprising had its roots in the overpowering of one cultural identity by another. Although plenty of evidence existed to illustrate the friendly interaction between Indians and settlers, there was, nevertheless, a growing undercurrent of resentment against white encroachment into the region. Much of the Indian land had been ceded away, with the Indians not having fared at all well in the exchange. Life on the reservation was poor, with no prospect of improvement. Food was scarce and the wild game was steadily disappearing. Government annuities were supposed to help, but often they were late and when they did finally arrive, the traders were right there to claim their share. A particular source of contention stemmed from a misunderstanding that surrounded the payment of these traders' debts. The Indians believed that the terms of the treaties included repayment of all monies owed the traders for credit that had been extended. The traders, however, insisted that they were still owed for credit given the Indians *after the treaties had been signed*.

In any case, as the decade of the 1860s began, conditions were ripe for trouble. A poor corn crop in 1861, followed by a severe winter, left the Santees in desperate need of food. A rapidly worsening situation was further exacerbated when federal annuity payments, which the Indians counted on to see them through, failed to arrive in June as scheduled, owing to a dilatory Congress and the financial demands of the Civil War. The Treasury Department could not decide whether to pay the overdue annuities in gold or paper money, the former being needed for the war effort, and the Indians suffered accordingly.

As the summer of 1862 progressed, the Sioux grew increasingly desperate. In mid-July, Agent Galbraith was confronted at the Upper Agency by angry Indians demanding to be fed, but he refused to release the goods in his warehouse until the annuity payments arrived. Trouble was averted by the presence of two companies of the Fifth Minnesota Infantry, under Lieutenants Timothy Sheehan and Thomas Gere, whom Galbraith had summoned when he feared trouble.

Two weeks later, on August 4, the Indians, this time not to be denied, surrounded Sheehan's camp and broke into the warehouse, helping themselves to the flour stored there. When Sheehan threatened them with two pieces of artillery they gradually backed down. Following this standoff, Sheehan contacted his superior at Fort Ridgely, Captain John Marsh, who arrived at the agency on August 6 and directed Galbraith to distribute the food and attempt to council with the Sioux leaders. As subsequent events were to demonstrate, however, the time for palaver had long since passed.

2

The Storm Breaks

Acton Township, Meeker County, Sunday, August 17, 1862

On August 17, two weeks after Captain Marsh managed to at least temporarily calm the horde of angry Indians at Upper Agency, the spark that finally ignited the uprising was struck at the home of one Robinson Jones, in Acton Township, Meeker County, near present Grove City. Jones and his wife operated a small combination store and post office on their homestead, some forty miles northeast of the Lower Agency. Here, on a pleasant Sunday, four young Indian men returning home to the Lower Agency from a hunt stopped at the Jones place. By name, the four were Brown Wing (Sungigidan), Breaking-Up (Ka-om-de-I-ye-ye-dan), Killing Ghost (Nagi-wi-cak-te), and Runs-Against Something When Crawling (Pa-zo-I-yo-pa). With Jones on this day were his two adopted children, together with two friends from Wisconsin. Mrs. Jones was visiting her son (from a first marriage), Howard Baker, at his farm, half a mile distant.

The hunt had not been a good one and the four Sioux were probably feeling frustrated. And they undoubtedly harbored resentment over the ill treatment at the hands of traders, to say nothing of the U.S. government's failure to provide promised annuities. In this frame of mind, they were operating with a short fuse, no longer in a mood to make any sort of distinction between traders, agents, and white settlers.

Whether the four were actually looking for trouble, or whether what followed was simply the natural progression of frustration to action, is a moot point. In any event, when one of the four was about to appropriate some eggs he had discovered, one of his friends reminded him that the eggs belonged to Jones. The reminder evidently angered the young Sioux, who then proceeded to smash the eggs and accuse his friend of cowardice for fearing to take something from a white man. The accused promptly denied his cowardice, saying he would confront Jones and shoot him, whereupon all four agreed to face the white man. Upon approaching Jones, the Indians demanded liquor, which was refused them. Having turned down the Indians' demand for liquor, Jones and his two friends decided to remove to the Baker place, leaving the children (ages fifteen and eighteen months) alone. The Indians chose to accompany the three adults to the Baker farm.

Monument on the site of the Baker farm where the Sioux uprising started

Clearly Jones did not perceive that the four Santees posed any real threat, else he would not have left the children alone. Upon arriving at the Baker place, Jones agreed to a shooting match with the four Sioux. The match, however, turned into a nightmare when the Indians suddenly fired on the whites, killing Jones and his wife, their two friends, and Howard Baker, before stealing some horses and heading for their village. The incident at the Baker farm, triggered by an act of bravado on this pleasant summer Sunday, was to prove the herald of a storm that would sweep down the valley of the Minnesota River. It was not planned, but given the existing conditions, it was perhaps inevitable.

The Indians Mobilize

When the four Indian hunters reached their Rice Creek village and related what had happened, there was immediate concern that the killings would bring down retribution. Some thought the four ought to be turned over to the white authorities, but others were ready to go to war, now that the first step had been taken. The village leader, Red Middle Voice, however, judged that the thing to do was to immediately head for the larger village of Chief Shakopee, eight miles away, and confer with him. Subsequently, these two leaders concluded that it would be unwise to go to war unless they could count on the support of the entire Lower Reservation, which would call for the backing of Little Crow, or Taoyateduta, perhaps the most prominent of the Santee leaders. If he was the most polished and eloquent spokesman of that group, Little Crow was also vain to a fault and, it was said, inordinately proud of his skills as a warrior.

Initially, Little Crow was opposed to war, as were several other leaders, who believed the Indians lacked the numbers and the resources to win such a war. It was not that

Little Crow was philosophically opposed to war with the whites, but he was a realist and appreciated the near impossibility of winning such a war. He seemed to have resigned himself and the fate of his people to an acceptance of the white man's way. He had embraced Christianity and was perceived by many whites as a friend. But suddenly, the picture had changed . . . dramatically. Now that the first step had been taken, others argued that the time had come to seek redress for the white man's wrongs. Then, too, most of the white soldiers were away, fighting their Civil War, so that mainly the Indians would only have to contend with volunteers, who had not impressed them with their soldierly qualities. If ever there was a time, it seemed, this was it.

After listening to the arguments, Little Crow at last and reluctantly agreed to lead his people in their war against the whites. Perhaps he yielded to the growing voice of those who sought action. Perhaps he, too, was finally caught up in this rising groundswell. The act of the four young braves had suddenly and unexpectedly brought Little Crow and the Santees to the brink of a Rubicon that, once crossed, could never be recrossed. In any case, tomorrow they would strike both reservation agencies.

The Lower Sioux Agency, Monday, August 18

Early on the morning of August 18 a large war party, probably 200 to 300 strong, gathered at the Lower Agency, where some 75 to 80 various agency employees were preparing for the day's work. When the signal was given, the Indians suddenly attacked. Esther Wakeman, a mixed-blood, described the onslaught that began the uprising. "Like a destructive storm, the war struck suddenly and spread rapidly. Everything was confusion. It was difficult to know who was friend and who was foe."[1]

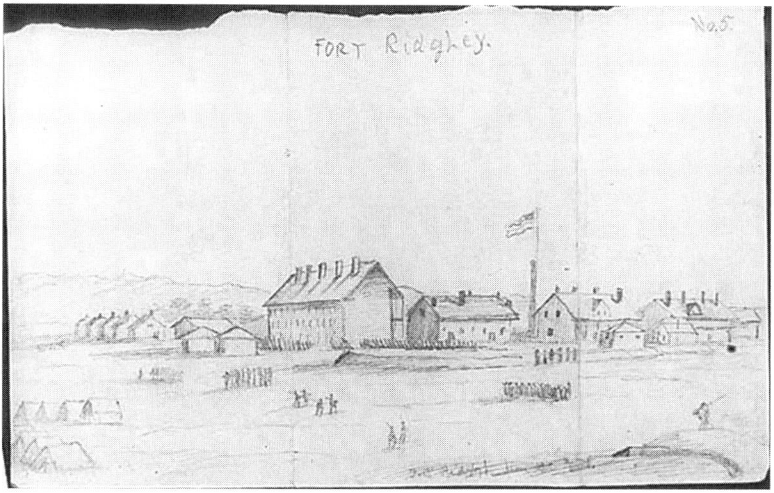

Sketch of Fort Ridgely

Among those who died in the early moments was the trader Andrew Myrick, who epitomized the uncaring and opportunistic trader. When asked by one of the agency interpreters earlier that month what the Indians were to eat if he did not extend credit to them, his reply was to let them eat grass. The body of trader Myrick was later discovered with grass stuffed in his mouth. Taken completely unawares, the whites offered little resistance. Some twenty were killed and another fifty taken captive as the rampaging Indians looted and burned. Some of the agency personnel did manage to escape across the river and head for Fort Ridgely, a dozen miles east.

Redwood Ferry, Monday, August 18

Captain John Marsh, commanding Company B, Fifth Minnesota Volunteers, at Fort Ridgely had learned of the

People escaping from the Indian outbreak of 1862

trouble at the Lower Agency from one of the survivors who reached the fort about midday. Soon, others began to arrive with tales of horror. Ironically, this very day a shipment of $71,000 in gold and silver, representing the Indians' annuity payment, had finally arrived at the fort, too late, obviously, to avoid the crisis; it was later returned to the Indian office in Washington.

Notwithstanding the stories he was hearing from survivors, Marsh was unconvinced that the trouble was all that serious. Nevertheless, he promptly organized a relief column of forty-six infantrymen and an interpreter and set out for the agency, leaving Lieutenant Thomas Gere and twenty-nine men at Fort Ridgely. At the same time, Marsh sent a message to Lieutenant Sheehan, commanding Company C, Fifth Minnesota, who had helped defuse a tense situation at the Upper Agency earlier in the month, to return to Ridgely as quickly as possible. Sheehan had departed the day before for Fort Ripley on the Upper Mississippi River; he would be no more than a day's march away.

Sheehan's fifty men were likely to be sorely needed.

Meanwhile, as Marsh's command was approaching Redwood Ferry, the Indians seized control of the ferryman's

Lieutenant
Timothy J. Sheehan

office, and others secreted themselves in the thickets bordering both sides of the river. As they approached the landing and were preparing to board the ferry, the troops were suddenly ambushed, with a dozen members of the command hit in the initial fusillade. In an effort to extricate the command, Marsh led his men through the protective cover of the brush, but soon found their way blocked by the attackers. Deciding then that the only way out was to cross the river, Marsh entered the water, his men following. Perhaps suffering from a cramp, Marsh began to struggle in the water and soon drowned, leaving it to nineteen-year-old Sergeant John Bishop to lead fifteen survivors back to Fort Ridgely. Twenty-four men, including Marsh, died in the Santee ambush, a nearly 50 percent loss.

The Upper Sioux Agency, Monday, August 18

Meanwhile, the situation at the Upper Agency had remained relatively quiet through the morning. By midday, however, scattered reports of attacks began to filter in

Location of Redwood Ferry where Captain Marsh and his men were ambushed and killed

to the agency, but most whites thought them exaggerated. Aside from those who had witnessed the horrors downriver—and somehow survived—few were prepared to believe the reports. Some of the Sioux at the Upper Agency began to think of joining the uprising, but others steadfastly opposed siding with the troublemakers at the Lower Agency. Of this latter group, none would prove more helpful to the whites than John Other Day, a Christianized Wahpeton Sioux who was married to a white woman and had a mixed-blood child. Although a number of Sioux had adopted Christianity, many quickly abandoned its teachings when the uprising burst into bright flame. John Other Day, however, stood firm in his adopted faith. He also, unlike the whites he took it upon himself to protect, recognized what was unfolding. Together with Joseph Laframboise, a French mixed-blood,

John Other Day managed to persuade many of the whites to take shelter in the brick warehouse, the largest and sturdiest of several agency buildings. That night rampaging Indians attacked nearby trading posts, but the agency proper was spared for the moment. At dawn Other Day led a group of sixty-two—some on foot, others riding in wagons—on a three-day trek to the relative safety of Cedar City, sixty miles distant. In retaliation, the angry Santees burned Other Day's farm. Later, the U.S. government, in recognition of his courage, awarded him $2,500 to replace it.

Two Christian missions located near the Upper Agency learned of the attacks through friendly Indians. Like others, they at first regarded the tales as exaggerated, but after visiting the abandoned agency they were persuaded otherwise. Some thirty of these folks banded together and made their way down the north shore of the Minnesota River to Fort Ridgely, managing somehow to avoid contact with roaming Sioux war parties.

Gabriel Renville, a thirty-seven-year-old mixed-blood who lived near the Upper Agency, later recalled the attack there:

> About three miles north of the agency there lived a white man who was a minister (Rev. Thomas S. Williamson). He was the first man who came among the Wahpetons to teach them, and was called the Doctor. He came out and met me, and asked what was being done and what the news was. I told him, "My friend, a great commotion has come. All the people at the Redwood Agency, and all the farmers across the river from that agency have been killed. But the people of the Yellow Medicine Agency, and the traders at that place, have all fled under the guidance of John Other Day last night."[2]

The Minnesota River Valley, Monday–Wednesday, August 18–20

All up and down the valley of the Minnesota River between New Ulm and the Upper Sioux Agency, a distance of some sixty miles, small farms and homesteads belonging mostly to German immigrant settlers found themselves feeling the heavy-handed wrath of the angry Sioux, who made little distinction among men, women, and children. Mostly the men were killed outright, as were many of the women and children, often in hideous fashion. Those who survived a brutal death were forced into captivity, with the women destined to be made wives. The death toll among settlers mounted rapidly: twenty-five in Renville County, fifty near Milford, twenty-six at Lake Shetek, and so on. Homesteads were looted and burned, the flames and smoke casting a pall of death and destruction throughout this normally tranquil valley.

In a few instances settlers were lulled into a fall sense of security by Indians they knew personally, who reassured them they would be protected, only to have the Indians suddenly turn on them. Some settlers came together and attempted to flee as a group only to be caught and either killed or taken prisoner. One, Samuel J. Brown, another mixed-blood, was a member of such a party and recalled how, after being made prisoners, they soon found four settlers who had not been as fortunate as themselves.

> We came upon four dead bodies—three men and one woman—all horribly mutilated. Our captors had committed the murders. The men had been mowing, and the woman had been raking hay. The scythes and pitchforks lay near—the woman had a pitchfork sticking in her person, and one of the men had a scythe sticking into his body. Cut Nose glee-

fully told me that he had killed this man and described how he did it. The man was mowing, he said, and he went up to him in a friendly manner and offered his hand, and as the white man threw down his scythe and reached out his hand the Indian drew his knife and like a flash plunged it into the white man's breast, just under the chin, whereupon the white man grasped him around the waist and both struggled for mastery, when they fell—the white man on top. In working the knife into his breast the Indian got his thumb into the white man's mouth and "got bit." The knife in the hands of the Indian soon touched a vital spot and the white man rolled off, dead.[3]

Fort Ridgely, Monday–Tuesday, August 18–19

With the loss of most of Captain Marsh's command in the ambush at Redwood Ferry, the garrison had been reduced to twenty-nine, of which seven were either ill or had been assigned to work in the hospital.

Faced with the stunning news of the disaster that had befallen Marsh, the post commander, nineteen-year-old Lieutenant Thomas P. Gere, now in charge of what remained of Fort Ridgely's garrison, prepared to defend the post with the limited forces at his disposal. The young officer was actually in no shape to command much of anything, having recently come down with the mumps. Gere's unenviable assignment was further complicated by the presence of thoroughly frightened settlers who continued to arrive, until by dark on this horror-filled day, some 250 had reached the very questionable safety of Fort Ridgely.

That night Gere wrote to Governor Alexander Ramsey and to the commanding officer at Fort Snelling. The letters were carried by Private William Sturgis, who set off on a long, 125-mile ride to the east (which he subsequently completed in the amazing time of eighteen hours). Realizing that he would need help sooner than could possibly be expected from his letters to the governor and Fort Snelling, Gere then sent off a second urgent message to Sheehan, imploring that officer to return as fast as possible; his fifty-man command was likely to be sorely needed.

> Force your march returning. Capt. Marsh and most of his command were killed yesterday at the Lower Agency. Little Crow and about 600 warriors are now approaching the fort and will undoubtedly attack us. About 250 refugees have arrived here for protection. The Indians are killing men, women and children.[4]

In the meantime, the tiny garrison and its flock of terrified settlers readied themselves for the attack, which seemed imminent. Gere ordered the women and children placed in the large stone barracks building and a defensive perimeter was established around the compound, using wagons, barrels, anything that might afford some protection for the defenders.

If the Sioux had launched a concerted attack when they arrived at the fort on the morning of the twentieth, they could easily have overrun the fort's few defenders. As it was, they convened a council of war, arguing over whether to attack Fort Ridgely or New Ulm. Little Crow and a handful of others who recognized the strategic value of eliminating the white man's military post in the heart of their country were overruled by the younger element, who saw more opportunities for plundering if they attacked the settlement of New Ulm, fifteen miles downriver. And so, unable to persuade the young warriors as to the importance of striking Fort Ridgely now, Little Crow had no choice but to acquiesce.

Barely had the Sioux departed when Lieutenant Sheehan arrived on the scene with his much-needed company. Being senior, Sheehan assumed command of the post, no doubt much to the sick Lieutenant Gere's great relief. Sheehan's arrival was followed by additional reinforcements in the form of fifty Renville Rangers, recently recruited to serve in the Civil War. Private Sturgis had encountered them en route to Fort Snelling and advised them of the situation. The Union army might have needed them in the east, but at the moment there was a greater need here at home, so the Rangers lost no time changing course to Fort Ridgely, which they reached on the evening of the nineteenth.

The arrival of Sheehan and the Rangers, together with some twenty-five armed civilians and the survivors of Marsh's command, who had returned from the ferry, increased the fort's garrison to about 180 men. Even though still greatly outnumbered, Sheehan's command was now in a position to put up a stout fight, precisely what Little Crow had feared would happen.

New Ulm, Monday–Tuesday, August 18–19

The community of New Ulm, built along the banks of the Minnesota River, was the largest in the area, having been founded by German colonists seven years earlier. Today New Ulm is a small but thriving community of 15,000, but in the summer of 1862 it was considerably smaller, with a population nearing 1,000.

News of the uprising had first reached New Ulm when young men from the area en route to join the Union army were attacked by a roving Indian war party. Survivors hastened back to the community to inform the inhabitants. If there was any doubt as to the seriousness of the situation,

The Dakotah House in New Ulm was used as a hospital during the Sioux Uprising.

that doubt was soon dispelled by the arrival of terror-stricken settlers, who reinforced the reports of the volunteers.

Despite the confusion that swept through the community, the inhabitants quickly managed to form a defense of sorts, led by the sheriff and a few others who possessed firearms, some military experience, or both. Some of those preparing to defend the community, however, were armed with nothing more than farm tools. Barricades were erected and women and children were put inside the town's largest buildings, while riders galloped out of town to seek assistance from surrounding communities.

By midday on August 19, more than 100 volunteers from the town of St. Peter, some twenty-five miles east, prepared to march to the aid of New Ulm. Shortly, the little citizen-army was joined by Charles S. Flandrau, former Indian agent and a well-known figure in Minnesota politics. While the relief column from St. Peter was readying itself, other, smaller groups of men, who had been alerted to the situation, headed for New Ulm, which, in the meantime, had been doing everything possible to prepare for the expected

Windmill at New Ulm. About twenty men occupied this structure located three blocks west of New Ulm's business district and held off the Indians in 1862.

Indian onslaught. It came about 3 P.M., when Indians began firing from high ground outside the town. The defenders returned the fire as best they could and a few even moved out from the town to carry the fight to the Indians. Had Little Crow and some of the other senior leaders, who were involved in the attack on Fort Ridgely, been present to provide guidance, the attack might have been more successful, but as it was, the effort lacked unity. Fortunately for the New Ulmers, as well, a strong thunderstorm moved into the area and put an end to the fighting. Later that night, Flandrau arrived from St. Peter at the head of his most welcome relief column. For the moment, New Ulm was secure, having suffered a dozen or so casualties and a few burned homes.

Fort Snelling, Tuesday, August 19

As events were unfolding in the Minnesota River Valley, word of the attacks reached Governor Alexander Ramsey,

Engraving depicting the attacks at New Ulm

who appointed Henry Hastings Sibley a colonel of volunteers and authorized him to respond to the uprising with military force. A powerful voice in the Minnesota legislature and one of the state's most respected individuals, Sibley was well-known to the Sioux; he had been a trader among them for nearly three decades and thus seemed the ideal man to take charge of the current situation. Sibley, however, lacked military experience and perhaps because of that he felt somewhat tentative in this new role.

To begin with, Sibley had at his immediate disposal four companies of the Sixth Minnesota—about 400 men—that were then in the process of organizing at Fort Snelling. With this force, Sibley promptly marched to St. Peter, where he received further word of Fort Ridgely's peril. The situation appeared to be worsening, so Sibley decided to await reinforcements and supplies before proceeding. During the next several days additional companies of the Sixth Minnesota arrived, augmented by companies of rangers and individual volunteers. When Sibley finally resumed his advance toward

Fort Ridgely, on August 26, it was with an army of some 1,400 men, which included about 400 mounted volunteers.

Fort Ridgely, Wednesday, August 20

Even as Sibley began his march toward the troubled area, Fort Ridgely was feeling the hand of war. Unsuccessful in his first attempt to strike the fort, Little Crow, in the twenty-four hours since, had managed to assemble a force of 400 warriors, some of whom had likely returned from their disappointing attack on New Ulm and were now ready to pay heed to Little Crow's counsel. Now that the war had started, he was determined to pursue a strategy that focused on the expulsion of the whites from his country, and the key to that was the taking of Fort Ridgely.

While a small party of warriors attempted a diversionary movement from the west, the main body, undetected, moved up through the ravines to the east, then attacked the northeast corner of the post. In this opening phase, Lieutenant Sheehan attempted to repulse the attack from a line of battle arranged on the parade ground, until several casualties forced the soldiers to take cover. But in return their fire forced the Indians to temporarily pull back.

A member of the Fort Ridgely garrison was John Jones, a regular army ordnance sergeant. Jones was an old artilleryman, who had been stationed here at Ridgely when the post was a field artillery school, during the late 1850s. Jones took pride in his profession as an artilleryman and, fortunately for the garrison at Fort Ridgely, he had made it a point of instructing the men in cannon drill. Now, in the face of the Indian attack, Jones's cannoneers methodically worked five field pieces, including a six-pounder, three twelve-pounders, and a twenty-four-pounder, and their fire kept the Indians pinned down in the ravines. By dark, Little Crow's warriors had had enough and withdrew toward the Lower Agency. That night, rain started to fall

Later photograph of Little Six (left) as a prisoner at Fort Snelling

and continued into the next day. Sheehan's garrison and the civilians used the respite to strengthen the fort's defenses as best they could and prepare for the next attack, which was certain to come.

Lightning Blanket, a Mdewakanton, recalled the Sioux attack on Fort Ridgely. His account is valuable in illuminating the weakness inherent in the Indian style of warfare against the whites.

> After reaching the Fort, the signal, three big shots (volleys), to be given by Medicine Bottle's men to draw the attention and fire of the soldiers, so the men on the east, Big Eagle's, and those on the west and south, Little Crow's and Little Six's could rush in and take the Fort.
>
> We reached Three-Mile creek before noon and cooked something to eat. After eating we separated,

I going with the footmen to the north, and after leaving Little Crow we paid no attention to the chiefs; everyone did as he pleased. Both parties reached the Fort about the same time, as we could see them passing to the west, Little Crow on a black pony. The signal, three big shots (volleys), was given by our side, Medicine Bottle's men, after the signal the men on the east, south, and west were slow in coming up. While shooting we run up to the buildings near the big stone one. As we were running in we saw the man with the big guns, whom we all knew and as we were the only ones in sight he shot into us, as he had got ready after hearing the shooting in our direction. Had Little Crow's men fired after we fired the signal[,] the soldiers who shot at us would have been killed.[5]

Notes

1. Gary Clayton Anderson, and Alan R. Woolworth, eds., *Through Dakota Eyes*, p. 55.
2. Ibid., p. 103.
3. Ibid., p. 77.
4. Fort Ridgely: *A Journal of the Past*, published by the Minnesota Historical Society, p. 2.
5. Anderson and Woolworth, *Through Dakota Eyes*, pp. 154–155.

3

The Uprising Spreads

In the three days since the attack on Robinson Jones's family near Acton, the effects of the uprising, though confined mainly to places immediately along the Minnesota River, were by no means limited to that area. Groups of Sioux fanned out to strike farms and small settlements well beyond the river. On August 20, for example, even as Little Crow's warriors were launching their first attack on Fort Ridgely, another war party struck the small Scandinavian settlement of West Lake, some forty miles northeast of the Upper Agency, killing fourteen.

Wednesday, August 20

Located some forty miles southwest of the Lower Agency, the Lake Shetek area had attracted a number of settlers since the area had been opened to settlement. It would prove to be the scene of much tragedy and suffering during the Minnesota uprising. A remarkable story of courage and heroism was also to emerge from the horror that befell this place.

John and Lavina Eastlick and their four children had a farm near Lake Shetek. With the arrival of daylight on the morning of Wednesday, August 20, the Eastlicks and other families in the Shetek area went about their normal daily chores, totally unmindful of the stark terror that had begun unfolding at the Lower Agency and elsewhere in the valley of the Minnesota River forty-eight hours earlier. There was concern among the area residents for the safety of Phineas Hurd and another man, who were en route from Fort Ridgely with provisions for the community. Ironically, the settlers' generosity in feeding the Indians this past winter had depleted their own stocks. Now, the settlers feared that some mishap had befallen the two men and elected to send a rider to Fort Ridgely for help in locating them.

Meanwhile, as the morning developed, a group of twenty Sioux rode up to the Hurd farm and after exchanging pleasantries with Alomina Hurd, suddenly unleashed one of the more horrid episodes of the entire uprising. After murdering the hired hand, the maddened warriors began a thorough and systematic destruction of the Hurds' home and possessions, afterward herding Mrs. Hurd and her children away from their now destroyed homestead. Death, she was certain, was imminent. But for some reason, totally out of character for them during these blood-crazed hours, the Indians suddenly abandoned Alomina and her children several miles down the trail.

By chance, a neighbor, Charley Hatch, arrived at the devastated homestead shortly after the Indians had left and discovered the grim scene. After recovering his composure, Hatch raced back to spread the alarm, but it was too late. Along the way, he bore witness to the killing of yet another neighbor, a man named Koch. Breathless, he reached the Eastlick place and reported what had happened.

Wasting no time, Hatch and the Eastlicks headed for the Wright place, being joined en route by the Smith family. The Wrights' home was large and sturdily built, offering the best protection of any structure in the area. Here, they found gathering a few other settlers who had learned of the trouble along with several longtime Indian friends, including one known as Old Pawn, who brought them up to date on the goings-on at the Lower Agency. Within eyeshot of the Wrights' home, Indians could clearly be seen burning and looting the Smith place. Knowing they were sure to be next, the little band of settlers prepared to defend themselves as best they could.

But some of the men thought they would do better to try to flee into the nearby woods before the Sioux war party—perhaps 200 strong—tired of destroying the Smith place and turned their attention to the Wright farm. And Old Pawn, too, saw this as their best chance. Accordingly, gathering everyone together, with the women and children in a wagon, the little party of settlers moved cautiously toward the woods, but they were soon under attack.

Seeking shelter in a large marshy area, the outnumbered whites fought back, but it was a hopeless situation. Fifteen whites perished in what would come to be known as "Slaughter Slough." Slowly, the Indians closed in on the terrified whites. The Indians promised that the women and children would not be harmed if they surrendered; otherwise the swamp would be fired. Faced with no other

Engraving depicting a white family murdered by Sioux Indians in Minnesota during the uprising

option, the women and children slowly emerged. The traitorous Old Pawn then informed two of the women that they were to be his wives. Squaws attacked one of the children and two other women were murdered while warriors laughed. Lavina Eastlick, carrying her small child and already wounded in the heel, was assured by Old Pawn that he would spare her life, only to then have him shoot her in the back. Before she was overcome by the pain of her wounds, she handed the baby to her eleven-year-old son, Merton. Shortly thereafter, perhaps having tired of the killing at "Slaughter Slough," the Indians abruptly pulled out.

Meantime, young Merton Eastlick and his brother Johnny had slipped back into the marshy area after the wounding of their mother. Their saga, however, was just beginning. Of all the stories to emerge from the terrible Minnesota uprising, none is more remarkable than that of the Eastlick brothers and their wounded mother.

After returning to "Slaughter Slough," Merton and Johnny joined up with the aged and badly wounded old Thomas Ireland, another member of the Lake Shetek community, known as "Uncle Tommy," who soon proved unable to continue and urged the boys to push on without him. And so began a remarkable journey of courage and determination. With no food and little water, eleven-year-old Merton plodded steadily onward, carrying fifteen-month-old Johnny on his back, always fearful of encountering more Indians. After traveling fifty miles, the brothers were miraculously reunited with their mother, Lavina, who had also survived, despite painful wounds. Together, the three continued on to Mankato and safety.

Fort Ridgely, Friday, August 22

Little Crow had been unsuccessful in his first attempt to destroy Fort Ridgely, but the failure by no means dissuaded him from a second effort. Indeed, he was more determined than ever to seize what he still regarded as the overall key to the uprising's success. Accordingly, forty-eight hours later, on August 22, the Sioux returned, this time with twice the strength, as an estimated 800 warriors moved against the post. After a barrage of fire arrows failed to ignite the wooden roofs, Little Crow decided to attack from the southwest, using his superior numbers to overpower the garrison. Led by Little Crow and Mankato, the Sioux surged toward the post. Their momentum carried them as far as the stables, where they released the livestock. But this proved their deepest penetration, as once again Sergeant Jones and his artillery, using well-placed salvos of canister and case-shot (hundreds of small iron or lead balls, with an effect much like that of a shotgun), to break up the attackers before they could reach the fort's main compound. In this effort, Jones was aided by Eliza Müller, wife of Fort Ridgely's surgeon, who helped the sergeant wheel his field piece into position. An unlikely hero of Fort Ridgely, Mrs. Müller not only helped Sergeant Jones, she also tended the sick and wounded and organized the other women in making ammunition from iron rods obtained from the blacksmith shop. By day's end, Little Crow, who was thought to have been wounded this day, elected to withdraw. The Sioux had had enough of Fort Ridgely, at least for the moment. Chief Big Eagle, who was present, later described the attack:

> But for the cannon I think we would have taken the fort. The soldiers fought us so bravely we thought there were more of them than there were. The cannons disturbed us greatly but did not hurt many. We did not have many Indians killed.[1]

New Ulm, Saturday–Sunday, August 23–24

Like Fort Ridgely, New Ulm was attacked twice. In the three days after the Indians' first attempt to take the town, the citizen defenders, under the overall command of Charles Flandrau, worked feverishly to strengthen the community's defenses. Additional reinforcements of other militia groups from Mankato and surrounding communities also arrived, raising Flandrau's command to some 300 defenders.

One of the ploys used by the Sioux was to trick the settlers into believing that all of the trouble was caused by their enemies, the Winnebagos, and now this rumor prompted nearly 100 of Flandrau's command to head back to their Blue Earth home, near the Iowa border, to deal with the Winnebagos who appeared to pose yet another threat in that area. Unfortunately, the remaining 200 or so men were not well armed and of course they lacked the discipline and training of a military command.

On Saturday, August 23, after creating a diversion in the direction of Fort Ridgely, which siphoned off nearly a third of Flandrau's command, some 650 Sioux, led by Wabasha, Mankato, and Big Eagle, attacked New Ulm from the west. As the Indians advanced, some defenders fell back, abandoning buildings that the Indians then occupied or set on fire. Fighting was furious; smoke from the burning buildings cast a grim pall over New Ulm. As the Indian advance swept forward, it wrapped around both flanks of the town like a giant pincer. Just as the Sioux were readying for a charge, Flandrau led a party on a counterattack, supported by fire from the rest of the defenders and driving the Indians out of the buildings they had occupied earlier. The maneuver, demonstrating once again that the best defense is sometimes to assume the offense, seemed to rob the Sioux of their initiative. Although they continued to exchange fire with the defenders until darkness, the

Indians, for all intents and purposes, seemed unwilling to press home the attack. By nightfall, the New Ulmers had suffered ninety-four casualties, more than a third of them deaths.

Sporadic firing resumed Sunday morning, at which time Flandrau and the other leaders decided to evacuate New Ulm. And so it was that the entire community, men, women, and children, all under the protection of the armed defenders, reinforced by an additional 150 new arrivals, began the twenty-five-mile trek downriver to Mankato. Necessarily slow-moving, the evacuees were vulnerable to attack at any moment, but, thankfully, reached their destination that night without further trouble.

Fight at Birch Coulee, September 2

Soon after Colonel Sibley arrived at Fort Ridgely on August 28, the mounted volunteers pulled out to return home and harvest their crops. Their departure not only reduced Sibley's effective fighting strength, it also left him with only a small contingent of cavalry and thus restricted his pursuit of the Indians. Overall, Sibley's volunteers were untrained and poorly armed and equipped. At Fort Ridgely the men were given some rudimentary basic training, while Sibley pleaded with Governor Ramsey for experienced troops and better weapons.

On August 31, reassured by scouts and local leaders that the Indians were no longer in the immediate area, Sibley organized a mixed force of infantry and cavalry, composed of the Sixth Minnesota under Captain Hiram Grant and the Cullen Guards, commanded by Captain Joseph Anderson, together with wagons and a handful of civilians, and sent them upriver to locate and bury soldiers and settlers who had been killed in the initial attacks. Command of the column was vested in Major Joseph Brown, former Indian agent and now an officer of volunteers.[2]

The column moved slowly upriver, stopping now and again to bury the bodies they came across. In all, some fifty corpses—men, women, and children—were found, badly decomposed from having been exposed to the elements for several days; many had been horribly mutilated without regard to age or gender. Sometimes the mutilations were in accord with traditional Sioux rituals for dealing with a vanquished foe. It was an orgy of slaughter, born out of hatred and disillusionment too long repressed, and in many instances fueled by plundered liquor. When the burial detail had completed its task, the column camped for the night near Birch Coulee Creek.

On the morning of September 1, Brown, with Captain Anderson and the cavalry, crossed to the south side of the river and proceeded upstream, burying the bodies of those slain at the Lower Agency. Grant and the infantry, meanwhile, continued along the north side of the river, burying the soldiers of Marsh's command who had perished in the ambush. Joseph Coursolle, a mixed-blood son of a French-Canadian trader and a Sisseton woman, accompanied the burial column and recalled the grisly task of burying bodies:

> The things we saw that day were too terrible to describe. Scattered along the road and at burned cabins we found the bodies of settlers, mostly men and boys. Fifty we buried before reaching the ferry. There the most gruesome sight of all awaited us. On the road lay the bodies of thirty-three young men [soldiers of Marsh's command] most of them in two files where they fell when the Sioux fired from almost point-blank range—killed in their tracks without returning a shot. All had been scalped and the uniforms had been stripped from their bodies. We dug at a furious pace in our haste to conceal the fearful sight.[3]

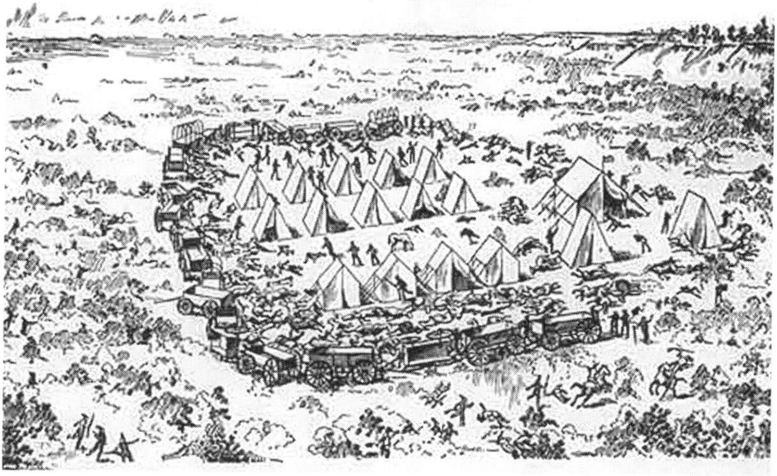

Engraving of the battle at Birch Coulee

After looking over the site of Little Crow's abandoned village, Brown crossed back to the north side of the river and rejoined Grant's detachment on the evening of September 1. Based on evidence found at Little Crow's old village and elsewhere along their route of march, the guides with the column were convinced that the Indians had not been in this area for perhaps three days. As a consequence, Brown was perhaps not as cautious as he might otherwise have been.

Brown's intelligence was mostly right; the Sioux had vacated the area, but only temporarily. Little Crow planned to assume the offensive once more, but before he did so, he decided to see that his women and children were moved out of harm's way. This done, on September 1, Little Crow, recovered sufficiently from his Fort Ridgely wound, personally led a war party toward the northeast, while a larger force of about 300 under Gray Bird moved back down along the south side of the Minnesota River, even as Brown's force was examining the same general area. Oddly, neither discovered the other.

The reunited command bivouacked at Birch Coulee. Like Fort Ridgely, Birch Coulee—now a state historic site—while offering water and wood, was ill-suited to a defensive stand, as the surrounding timber and gullies allowed an undetected approach. The poor choice of a campsite indicated Brown's lack of concern as to the presence of Indians. "Don't worry about Indians," Brown told his men. "You're just as safe as if you were home in your own beds!"[4] But Gray Bird's war party was indeed present. During the night, the Sioux crossed the Minnesota River and surrounded the camp.

At dawn, a guard noticed movement on the periphery of the camp and opened fire, which was immediately returned by the Indians. The soldiers suffered some thirty casualties in this opening exchange, as Brown, Grant, and Anderson quickly attempted to form a defensive position. Many of the soldiers used horses killed in the initial fusillade as barricades, while others attempted to dig rifle pits. Twenty-nine-year-old Joseph Coursolle recalled their shock and predicament when the Indians attacked:

> Most of us were asleep when the firing started and for a time we didn't know what was happening. Some men stood up to form a firing line but soon flopped down on their bellies like the rest. All of us had turned in for the night with muskets loaded, so we returned the fire before the warriors reached the wagons. . . . There were nearly a hundred horses on the picket ropes and many of them were hit by the first volley the Indians fired. Some dropped dead and others broke loose and galloped terror-stricken in the wagon enclosure.[5]

Again, the Indians might well have overrun the army position, but seemed content to remain in position and

The battle at Birch Coulee

maintain a steady fire on the besieged troops. As the sound of gunfire carried downriver to Fort Ridgely, Sibley wasted no time dispatching a relief column of 250 men of the Sixth Minnesota, some rangers, and artillery, all under Colonel Samuel McPhail. However, as McPhail marched toward the sound of the guns, his force was confronted by a war party that the colonel imagined to be much larger than it actually was. Halting, he sent Lieutenant Sheehan back to Ridgely carrying a request for reinforcements, which brought Sibley himself out with the remainder of his command, seven companies of infantry. After uniting with McPhail, the combined force moved forward, albeit cautiously, toward Birch Coulee. As they approached Brown's encircled troops on the morning of September 3, Sibley's artillery soon scattered the Sioux and ended the siege, which had been a costly one for Brown's command. Thirteen people were killed and forty-seven wounded. After burying the dead, Sibley's command returned to Fort Ridgely.

Little Crow Attacks Meeker County, September 1–2

While Brown's burial column was fighting for its life at Birch Coulee, some forty crow-flight miles to the northeast, Little Crow led a party of 100 warriors toward communities in Meeker County, an area perceived as being ripe for plundering. En route, however, just as at Fort Ridgely back on August 18, a disagreement arose as to which target should be struck first. The bulk of the war party, about seventy-five strong, under Walker-Among-Sacred-Stones, split off from the rest, leaving Little Crow with about thirty-five warriors. On the night of September 1, the big group camped about two miles northeast of the Acton township farm of Robinson Jones, where the whole bloody uprising had begun on August 17. Little Crow's party, meanwhile, camped an equal distance southeast of the Jones farm.

Even as the Indian war party was moving toward Meeker County, some fifty men of the Tenth Minnesota, together with about half as many civilians, reached the Jones farm. This contingent, under the command of Captain Richard Strout, had been sent to provide protection to the citizens of Meeker County.

Those in the area had learned of an Indian presence when militia from Forest City, about seven miles north of Litchfield, had a scrape with the Sioux on September 1. Whether these were from the Little Crow war party or a smaller, independent group is not clear, but in any case, Forest City, at least, was on the alert. The same could not be said, however, for Strout's command. Fortunately, they were made aware of the situation by messengers sent from Forest City.

On the morning of September 3, Strout, having prepared his command, moved west, and clashed with Little Crow's warriors at Hope Lake (about seven miles south of Litchfield, now on Route 1). The two sides were about evenly matched in number until the main body of Sioux warriors, having heard the sounds of battle, arrived on the scene. Despite being relatively new recruits, Strout's men acquitted themselves well: for a time it was *mano a mano*, with the soldiers finally using bayonets to break through the Indian lines and carry out a fighting withdrawal to the town of Hutchinson, some twenty miles southeast. The fight cost Strout heavily. Of his original force of fifty-five, six were dead and at least fifteen wounded, a casualty rate of 38 percent.

The following day, Little Crow, further reinforced by the arrival of another small body of warriors, divided his force for a twin strike at both Forest City and Hutchinson. Much to the Indians' frustration, however, both settlements had erected small fortress-like structures to provide protection for the citizens, and from which the defenders were able to turn back repeated attacks. In the end, Little Crow's warriors were forced to settle for destroying whatever they could find outside the stockades before finally withdrawing from the area, no doubt mightily chagrined at their failure to destroy either community.

The Plight of the Captives

Although the death toll grew frightfully along with the plundering and destruction, not all settlers who found themselves at the mercy of the Sioux were killed. Many, especially women, were taken prisoner. Some were raped on the spot, then killed, while others were taken to become some warrior's future wife. It was a curious kind of war—and that seems like a fair way to describe the events of 1862. In some instances, stunned settlers suddenly found themselves confronted by angry demoniacal fiends with whom they'd broken bread or shared the same church pew but a day or two before. For some, that relationship made the difference between life and death; for others it did not matter.

Mrs. Joseph Brown, a Sioux woman who had married a white trader, was personally protected by Little Crow. George Spencer, a clerk, was one of the few men taken captive at the Lower Agency and survived captivity because of his friendship with a Sioux named Chaska.

Those taken into captivity were ultimately brought to the Indian village, where some were subjected to further indignities, including rape, menial labor, and beatings. A few fortunate souls were sheltered by friendly Indians, but all were faced with the dreadful imagery of what ultimate fate awaited them.

Nancy McClure Faribault Huggan was one of those who survived the ordeal of her captivity. The daughter of an army officer and a Dakota, the twenty-five-year-old woman was captured, along with her husband and eight-year-old daughter, at their home near the Redwood or Lower Agency. Upon the approach of the Indians, the family hid in the nearby woods, and was joined there by Louis Brisbois, a mixed-blood, and his family. The Indians knew they were there, however, and promised not to harm them if they surrendered. At length, the settlers elected to surrender and take the Indians at their word. The promise of safety, it seems, did not extend to Brisbois and his family. Nancy Faribault Huggan recalled the terror of that day:

> The Indians at once disarmed my husband. They seemed a little surprised to see the Brisbois family, and declared they would kill them, as they had not agreed to spare their lives. Poor Mrs. Brisbois ran to me and asked me to save her, and she and her husband got behind me, and I began to beg the Indians not to kill them. My husband asked the Indians what all this meant—what they were doing anyhow. They replied, "We have killed all the white people at the agency; all the Indians are on the warpath; we are going to kill all

the white people in Minnesota; we are not going to hurt you, for you have trusted us with goods, but we are going to kill these Brisbois." And then one ran up and struck over my shoulder and hit Mrs. Brisbois a cruel blow in the face, saying she had treated them badly at one time. Then I asked them to wait until I got away, as I did not want to see them killed. This stopped them for half a minute, when one said: "Come to the house." So we started for the house, and just then two more wagons drawn by oxen and loaded with white people came along the road. All the Indians left us and ran yelling and whooping to kill them. . . . The white people were nearly all murdered. I could not bear to see the sickening sight. When the killing was over, the Indians came to the house and ordered us to get into one of the wagons and go with them back to the agency. . . . When we reached the agency there was a dreadful scene. Everything was in ruins, and dead bodies lay all about. . . . We did not stay long here, but pushed on to Little Crow's camp. We stayed that night with the Indians that brought us. Soon other prisoners, many of them half-bloods like ourselves, were brought in.[6]

The Refugees

In all, nearly 300 white settlers and mixed-bloods were taken captive by the rampaging Sioux, but hundreds of others—singly and in small and large groups—managed, somehow, to avoid the bloody swath of terror that spread up and down the valley of the Minnesota River and beyond like a wildfire. As with the captives, theirs were accounts of courage, hardships, and great perseverance. Of these, the ordeals of young Merton Eastlick and his mother, Lavina, along with those of Alomina Hurd and her children, all survivors of the Lake Shetek tragedy, stand out as triumphs of the human spirit.

Little Crow Fails to Unite the Santee Sioux Bands

From the outset, Little Crow had sought the participation of the Indian bands at the Upper Agency, albeit with little success. A pair of attacks on both Fort Ridgely and New Ulm had failed, but would almost certainly have succeeded had the Upper Agency bands joined forces with them. Then, when news came that their old friend, Henry Sibley, was marching against them, Little Crow abandoned his camp—warriors, women, and children, together with some 250 captives—and moved upriver to the Yellow Medicine Agency, where he hoped to persuade the Sissetons and Wahpetons to join forces with him. But most of these Upper Agency Indians were of a different mind-set and refused the overtures of Little Crow and his followers. As far as the Upper bands were concerned, this was not their war and they wished no part of it.

Paul Mazakutemani, son of a Wahpeton woman and a Mdewakanton man, addressed the Upper Agency bands:

> Sissetons, the Mdawakontons have made war upon the white people, and have now fled up here. I have asked them why they did this, but I do not yet understand it. I have asked them to do me a favor, but they have refused. Now I will ask them again in your hearing. Mdawaktons, why have you made war on the white people? The Americans have given us money, food, clothing, ploughs, powder, tobacco, guns, knives, and all things by which we

> might live well; and they have nourished us even like a father his children.

Paul Mazakutemani was also most distressed over the plight of the captives and asked to have them released to him.

> Give me all these white captives. I will deliver them to their friends. You Dakotas are numerous—you can afford to give these captives to me, and I will go with them to the white people. Then, if you want to fight, when you see the white soldiers coming to fight, fight with them, but don't fight with women and children.[6]

Despite Mazakutemani's pleas and exhortations, however, Little Crow's followers refused to surrender the captives, vowing that if they must die, so, too, would the captives. Heated words were exchanged between the two groups of Sioux, but in the end, Little Crow would have to win this war with his Lower Agency followers.

Notes

1. Anderson and Woolworth, *Through Dakota Eyes*, p. 149.
2. Brown's title of major was not a military rank. Indian agents traditionally were given the honorary title of major.
3. Anderson and Woolworth, *Through Dakota Eyes*, p. 161.
4. Ibid., p. 162.
5. Ibid., p. 162.
6. Ibid., pp. 83–84.
7. Ibid., pp. 196–197.

4

Retribution and Salvation

As word of the uprising gradually spread, communities made preparations to defend themselves. Throughout central and southern Minnesota, from Little Falls and St. Cloud on the north to the Iowa border on the south, communities like St. Joseph, Glencoe, and Sauk Center (future home of novelist Sinclair Lewis) quickly erected various blockhouse-type structures, from which colorfully titled home guardsmen such as the "Frontier Avengers," "LeSueur Tigers," and "Cullen Guards" stood ready to repel any attack. It was reminiscent of eighteenth-century conditions in New England and along the Ohio River frontier.

Beyond the communities themselves, the wheels of the state and federal governments had finally begun to turn. In St. Paul, Governor Alexander Ramsey, not content to rely on Colonel Sibley's small army to restore order, set in motion the machinery to create a state militia. On September 3, he appointed Charles Flandrau a colonel, with orders to take charge of the state's southern defense system. Flandrau created a line of defensive structures extending southwest from New Ulm to the Iowa state line, where the Iowa Northern Border Brigade had built a fort in the aftermath of the infamous 1857 Spirit Lake Massacre perpetrated by the renegade Wahpekute Sioux, Inkpaduta, or Scarlet Point.

Following the Spirit Lake strike of terror, Little Crow's people had been charged with the responsibility of capturing Inkpaduta or risking the loss of their annuities. The government soon wisely rescinded this decision, but the order did not sit well with the Santees, nor should it have. Inkpaduta, though a Wahpekute, was a brigand and outcast, not a legitimate member of either the Upper or Lower Agency. Nevertheless, Little Crow's people undertook the mission of finding Inkpaduta, but that wily miscreant and his followers slipped away into the vastness of the Dakota Territory beyond the Missouri River, where eventually he would ally himself with the Teton Lakota Sioux of Sitting Bull and Crazy Horse. At any rate, even though the Bureau of Indian Affairs backed away from its original threat to withhold annuities, the Inkpaduta affair may properly be regarded as another cause of the resentment that served as the basis for the 1862 uprising.

At the federal level, things were also happening. Recognizing, at last, the seriousness of the troubles in

General John A. Pope

Minnesota, President Abraham Lincoln, on September 6, appointed Major General John Pope to command the newly created Department of the Northwest, comprising the states of Minnesota, Iowa, Wisconsin, Nebraska, and the Dakota Territory. A controversial commander, Pope, who had perhaps been unfairly sacked after the Second Battle of Bull Run, was not lacking in military ability, especially to hear him tell of it. Although initially bitter over being relegated to what he considered a backwater command, Pope was persuaded as to the importance of the assignment and once on the scene promptly went to work to end the uprising. "Take such prompt and vigorous measures as shall quell the hostilities," Pope directed Sibley.

Although Pope lost no time clamoring for more men and equipment, with the Civil War raging from the Atlantic seaboard to the Mississippi, there were few troops to be spared. So the task of quelling the uprising and defending the frontier rested largely on the shoulders of the hastily formed volunteer regiments, together with the various units of local militia.

In addition to men and equipment, a big challenge confronting Pope was the acquisition of horses for cavalry. There were a number of mounted militia detachments serving at various locations on the Minnesota frontier, but they were deemed essential for local defense and thus were not available to Sibley. By the end of the year, Sibley would have a thousand mounted troopers in his command, but here and now, as he prepared to advance from Fort Ridgely, he had but twenty-five mounted men.

The Chippewa Threat

While the authorities sought to deal with the uprising, concern also grew for lives and property farther north and east, in the St. Croix River Valley. As always in troubled times, rumors were plentiful and settlers worried that the

Chippewa (Ojibway), whose homeland was the Mississippi and St. Croix River Valleys, were going to join their traditional enemies the Sioux in driving whites out of Minnesota. If the fear was exacerbated by the troubles in the Minnesota River Valley, neither was it entirely without basis. As a matter of fact, on August 18, even as the Santees were rampaging through the Lower Agency and ambushing Captain Marsh's command, Major Lucius Walker, agent at Crow Wing Agency, located near the confluence of the Mississippi and Crow Wing Rivers, heard an alarming report that the Chippewa, under a troublesome leader named Hole-in-the-Day, were preparing for war.

After requesting military assistance from Fort Ripley, some seven miles south of the agency, Walker, a victim of fear and paranoia, fled south out of harm's way. So disturbed was he over an outbreak he may have imagined himself to be responsible for, Walker later committed suicide.

With Lieutenant Timothy Sheehan and fifty men helping out at Fort Ridgely, the Fort Ripley garrison had been reduced to thirty-five men. Nevertheless, upon receipt of Walker's request for assistance, a detachment of twenty soldiers under the command of Lieutenant Frank Fobes moved north. En route they met the fleeing Walker, who ordered Fobes to arrest Hole-in-the-Day, who, however, managed to elude the soldiers and escape.

Meanwhile, and coincidentally, the U.S. commissioner of Indian Affairs, William Dole, on his way to the area near present-day Grand Forks, North Dakota, to negotiate a treaty with two bands of Chippewas, learned of the trouble from Agent Walker. After first returning to St. Paul for a conference with Governor Ramsey, Dole headed back to Fort Ripley with two companies of infantry, hoping to smooth things out with Hole-in-the-Day. Dole's efforts, however, led to mostly naught, save for the return of some stolen property. At length, Dole departed, putting on hold any treaty talk with the Chippewas and leaving an interim agent to see to a resolution of the problem. Although Hole-in-the-Day and his band appeared ready to take the warpath, he failed to garner much support from the other Chippewa leaders, and with the army presence now reinforced to three companies of infantry, the Chippewa threat soon fizzled.

Fort Abercrombie, September 3–29

Of the Minnesota forts, Ridgely and Abercrombie were subjected to fierce attacks during the 1862 uprising, and in the case of Abercrombie, to a twenty-six-day siege. In 1862, Ripley, Ridgely, and Abercrombie were all garrisoned by the Fifth Minnesota Infantry: Company C at Fort Ripley, Company B at Fort Ridgely, and Company D at Abercrombie, where the commander was a distinguished-looking, thirty-one-year-old former grocer from St. Paul, Captain John Vander Horck. Like most others in the Fifth Minnesota, he had no military experience to prepare him for his new assignment. When Vander Horck took command of Fort Abercrombie, Company D totaled approximately eighty men.

Shortly after Vander Horck took over Fort Abercrombie, a wagon train of supplies, accompanied by a cattle herd, reached the fort en route to the site of the treaty talks Commissioner Dole had originally planned before the interruption by Hole-in-the-Day. But when Vander Horck learned of the Indian uprising through a newspaper article, he promptly ordered the wagon train brought back to the fort and recalled thirty soldiers who had been sent fifty miles downstream on detached duty.

As word of the uprising spread, settlers from the surrounding area sought protection at the fort, which, like Fort Ridgely, was not designed to repel attackers. Not only that, but the troops did not even have the right ammunition for their muskets. Vander Horck had repeatedly asked for the right ammunition, but thus far to no avail. Now he sent an urgent request to Governor Ramsey for reinforcements as well.

As one by one the days of August passed uneventfully, patrols from the fort found no Indian activity, but did discover several mutilated bodies. To the garrison of Fort Abercrombie and the settlers who had fled to the fort for safety, there seemed no question but that the Sioux would strike any day. Then on August 30, a war party ran off the livestock herd. Although the Sioux made no effort against the fort on this occasion, it foreshadowed things to come.

Four days later, on September 3, the Indians launched their first attack against the fort. Earlier that morning, while inspecting his defenses, Vander Horck had been wounded by a jittery sentinel and was temporarily rendered *hors de combat*. Despite the absence of its commander, though, the garrison responded vigorously and with the support of cannon fire drove off the attackers after some two hours of hard fighting.

Fortunately for the garrison, the Santees chose not to launch a second attack immediately. The welcome hiatus allowed the garrison—including the women of the post—to rob the artillery canister shells of their steel shot for use in the infantry muskets. The Indians, of course, had no knowledge of the fort's inadequate ammunition supply, but even had plenty of ammunition been available, a concerted follow-up effort would almost certainly have resulted in the capture of the fort. Admittedly, Abercrombie, because of its location, was not as important as Fort Ridgely, but its capture would nevertheless have been a giant coup.

As it was, the Indians did not resume their attack until September 6. This time more warriors joined in the attack, perhaps as many as 200, nearly twice the number who had attacked on the third, prompting the defenders to speculate that warriors from the Upper Agency had now joined Little Crow's Lower Agency army. The Upper Sioux, however, later claimed not to have been involved. In any event, this second attack, like the first, was broken up by determined fighting on the part of the defenders and their artillery support. The scenario at Fort Abercrombie was similar to that at Fort Ridgely: stubbornness on the part of the defenders, backed up by artillery.

An anxious Vander Horck must have daily scanned the approaches from the south, not knowing whether the messengers carrying his pleas for reinforcements and ammunition had ever reached Governor Ramsey, but undoubtedly hoping that they had gotten through. Indeed they had. Even as the Santees were launching their attack of September 6, a relief column of sixty men, under the command of Captain Emil Buerger, started from St. Paul. Along the way they were joined by additional units, so that by the time they reached Fort Abercrombie on September 23, the column numbered some 450 men. Although there were fights with the Indians on the twenty-sixth and again on the twenty-ninth of September, the arrival of Buerger's column effectively ended the siege of Fort Abercrombie.

Sibley Returns to Action

Following the fight at Birch Coulee back on September 2, Colonel Sibley had wanted to resume his campaign, but he had been convinced that his command needed shoring-up before he advanced. As a consequence, he had continually asked Governor Ramsey for more men, equipment, and horses. Many of his cavalry mounts had died in the Birch Coulee fight, leaving the colonel with virtually no mounted force. Besides that, he badly needed trained troops. In any case, Sibley was not yet prepared to take the field.

While he awaited the arrival of reinforcements and supplies, and while the troops on hand were drilled and trained, it occurred to Sibley that perhaps Little Crow might be ready to negotiate. Perhaps the whole bloody business could be brought to an end without further fighting. There was some reason to be hopeful in this regard, as some of the Indian leaders seemed disposed to give up, but they and their followers were in the minority. Although Little Crow seemed willing to discuss the situation, he stubbornly refused to release the captives and as far as Sibley was concerned, this was a non-negotiable point.

In view of this, Sibley planned to resume the campaign just as quickly as his command proved ready, and by mid-September that time seemed close at hand. Ammunition and supplies had arrived, as had reinforcements: nearly 300 veterans of the Third Minnesota who had been captured at the Battle of Murfreesboro, Tennessee, paroled, and sent home to fight Indians. Altogether, Sibley now had more than 1,600 men of the Third, Sixth, Seventh, and Ninth Minnesota, plus local citizen-soldiers and some artillery.

The Battle of Wood Lake, September 23

At long last, on September 19, more than two weeks after the Birch Coulee fight, Sibley moved out of Fort Ridgely and resumed his advance up the Minnesota River Valley. Four days later, on September 22, the column reached a small body of water then known as Lone Tree or Battle Lake.

Sibley's intelligence had reported the Sioux to be located much farther up the valley and, as a result, the colonel did not feel a need to be particularly vigilant insofar as camp security was concerned. Completely unbeknownst to him, however, Little Crow had slipped down from the north with more than a thousand warriors, craftily planning to waylay Sibley's column when it resumed the march on September 23. Here, as at Birch Coulee, an assumption that the enemy was not close by nearly proved fatal. In Sibley's case, only an act of serendipity saved him from an acute embarrassment, or perhaps worse.

On the morning of the twenty-third, a party of the Third Minnesota decided to take an unauthorized journey to the Upper Agency, there to scrounge for a few potatoes to enliven their otherwise dismal rations. The trip, however illegal, proved a blessing, because as the soldiers made their way across the prairie, they inadvertently stumbled upon Little Crow's warriors, waiting in concealment to ambush Sibley's column when it resumed the march.

Their strategy now foiled, accidentally or not, the Indians opened fire on the soldiers, wounding some. The other soldiers, recovering, returned the fire. Meanwhile, back at the bivouac area, the remainder of the Third Minnesota promptly advanced toward the sound of the guns, doing so without orders, even as had their comrades (on this campaign, at least, the Third Minnesota seems to have regarded itself as an independent command). As the Third advanced, the Indians retired, but in doing so, began to spread out left and right, so as to threaten Sibley's flanks.

As Sibley watched this fight, which he had not initiated, take on a life of its own, he quickly perceived the threat to his flanks and directed the Seventh Minnesota to counter the threat on the right, supported by fire from the column's

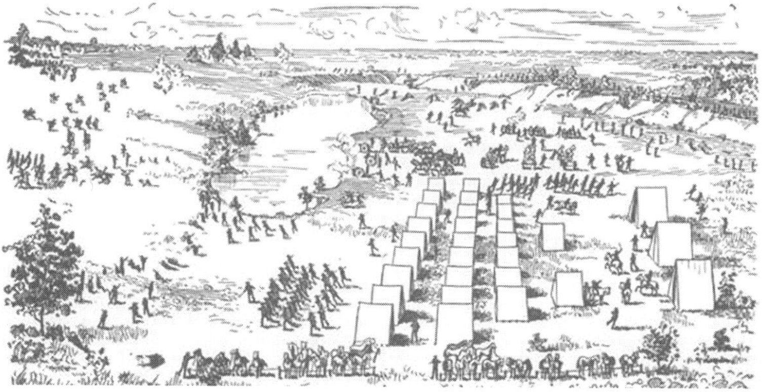

The battle of Wood Lake

six-pounder howitzer. On the left flank, the remainder of the Seventh Minnesota, reinforced by a company from the Sixth, turned back the Indian effort. After two hours, more or less, the Santees had had enough. They had lost their opportunity to strike Sibley's force by surprise and had suffered a number of casualties, including the death of the influential Chief Mankato.

Sibley described the battle in his after-action report:

> About 7 o'clock this morning [September 23] the camp was attacked by about 300 Indians, who suddenly made their appearance and dashed down toward us whooping and yelling in their usual style and firing with great rapidity. The Renville Guards under Lieutenant Gorman was sent by me to check them, and Major Welch of the Third Regiment, was instantly in line with his command, his skirmishers in the advance, by whom the savages were gallantly met and, after a conflict of a serious nature, repulsed. Meantime another portion of the Indian force passed down a ravine, with a view to outflank the Third Regiment, and I ordered Lieutenant-Colonel Marshall, with five companies of the Seventh Regiment, who was ably seconded by Major Bradley, to advance to its support with one 6-pounder, under the command of Captain Hendricks, and I also ordered two companies of the Sixth Regiment to reinforce him. Lieutenant-Colonel Marshall advanced at a double-quick amid a shower of balls from the enemy, which fortunately did little damage to his command, and after a few volleys he led his men to a charge and cleared the ravine of savages. Major McLaren, with Captain Wilson's company, took position on the extreme left of the camp, where he kept at bay a party of the enemy who were endeavoring to gain the rear of the camp and finally drove

> them back. The battle raged for about two hours, the 6-pounder and the mountain howitzer being used with great effect, when the Indians, repulsed at all points with great loss, retired with precipitation.[1]

Interestingly, the so-called fight at Wood Lake is misnamed. When Sibley's column reached the general area where the fight occurred, the courageous John Other Day, who had returned to Fort Ridgely to offer his services to Sibley as guide, apparently mistook Lone Tree Lake for Wood Lake, which is actually three miles to the west. Thus, the affair came to be known as the Battle of Wood Lake, rather than the Battle of Lone Tree Lake, where it was actually fought. Today, Lone Tree Lake no longer exists.

Sibley did not immediately pursue, giving as an explanation that he lacked cavalry, which was true enough, and a strong mounted force was essential in pursuing an Indian war party. Sibley instead chose to see that his dead were buried and his casualties were cared for. The delay also enabled him to ponder his next move. Sibley had to bear in mind the fate of the captives. His objective, therefore, had to be not only the unconditional surrender of the militant Santees, but also the safe retrieval of the captives.

Surrender of the Santees, Release of the Hostages, September 26

On the face of it, the Battle of Wood Lake would appear to have been inconclusive, but in fact, it marked the end of the uprising in terms of military action in Minnesota. However, the summer's madness would lead to extended campaigns in Dakota in 1863 and again in 1864 (see Epilogue).

For Little Crow, Wood Lake was the nadir of a failed effort to restore the dignity of his people by driving the white man out of Minnesota and bringing back the old ways. The voices of those opposed to a continuance of the uprising grew ever louder and now included some from among his own followers. However, the opposition remained strongest among those bands from the Upper Agency, who had not only refused to side with Little Crow's faction from the start, but continued to argue for the release of the captives.

Known as "friendlies" because of their attitude toward the captives and their opposition to the uprising, these bands of Santees indirectly proved a powerful ally of the whites. The Wahpeton chief Red Iron threatened to attack Little Crow's army if it encroached on his territory. Indeed, it almost came to that. During the fighting at Wood Lake, with the militants otherwise occupied, the "friendlies" took it upon themselves to transfer the captives from Little Crow's camp to their own near the confluence of the Chippewa and Minnesota Rivers. Having

Three survivors of the Sioux uprising: Mary E. Schmidt, Helen M. Carrothers, Maria White

done this, they sent one of the mixed-blood captives to Sibley with a message to the effect that the captives were now safe.

Armed with the reassurance that the captives were out of danger, Sibley resumed his northward march on the morning of September 25, reaching the camp of the "friendlies" that afternoon. Sibley arrived at the camp with great pomp. Seventeen-year-old Samuel J. Brown, a mixed-blood captive, vividly recalled the moment:

> No grander sight ever met the eyes of anybody than when the troops marched up with bayonets glistening in the bright noon day sun and colors flying, drums beating and fifes playing. I shall never forget it while I live. We could hardly realize that our deliverance had come. The troops passed by and pitched their tents a quarter of a mile from us and at once spiked their guns which commanded our camp.[2]

After a brief parley, some 150 mixed-bloods and ninety-one white captives were turned over to Sibley. An additional twenty-eight captives were released over the next few days, bringing the total to 269, of which 107 were white and the remainder, 162, mixed-blood. The soldiers of Sibley's command promptly and appropriately enough named the site Camp Release, which is today a state monument, marked by a fifty-foot shaft that memorializes the moment when 269 captives had their freedom restored. Some of the captives were taken to Fort Ridgely; orphaned children were sent to the settlements to be cared for. Some women who had been held captive were detained at Sibley's camp for a time to help identify Sioux prisoners who might be charged with crimes. Nancy McClure Faribault Huggan remembered that "at last a lot of us released captives were started off for the settlements below. There were seven wagon loads of us in the party, whites and mixed-bloods, all women."[3]

Little Crow and his followers had, meanwhile, begun to exit the Minnesota country. The uprising was finished, and for those who refused to surrender to the soldiers the only path open was west, into Dakota Territory, where they hoped to find support from their Yankton and Teton brethren.

For Little Crow himself it had been a humiliating experience. "I am ashamed to call myself a Dakota," he pronounced, following Wood Lake. "Seven hundred of our best warriors were whipped yesterday by the whites. Now we had better all run away and scatter out over the plains like buffalo and wolves."[4]

Little Crow had initially been opposed to the uprising, but once committed, he sought total victory with all the skills he possessed. Despite his considerable influence and prestige, however, he was unable to unify the Upper and Lower Sioux in pursuit of a common goal, and that failure probably hurt the uprising more than any other single factor. And, even among those he led, Little Crow found that he lacked sufficient support to prosecute the uprising in accordance with the grand strategic view proposed by himself and a few other leaders. Lost opportunities at Fort Ridgely and New Ulm, in particular, undermined the uprising, which had been initiated on a highly emotional note to begin with. Without any solid victories to sustain the movement, it steadily lost momentum. Sadly, the uprising, despite its heavy cost, led to no lasting reforms and did not address the issues that led to the uprising in the first place. Although the Minnesota River Valley soon returned to normal, it would never be quite the same for the generation that experienced the terror of that August; the sense of permanency was gone forever.

Indian jail for Sioux uprising captives

Scene in prison where Indians await U.S. government decision

Retribution, December 26, 1862

Sibley remained at Camp Release for a month, getting under way with the complicated process of dispersing captives and separating the suspected guilty Indians from the nonguilty. Initially, there were an estimated 1,200 Santees in or immediately about what came to be called Camp Release. That number rose steadily, as an increasing number of Indians either were brought in by army patrols or came in of their own accord. By the end of October, Sibley reported that he had nearly 500 "in irons" or being carefully watched. Eventually, the camp contained some two thousand Indians, plus Sibley's 1,600-man army, all of whom needed to be fed. To ease the

The courthouse used by the military commission

logistical burden, some of the Santees were sent to gather what crops might still remain from the fields around the Upper Agency. Army patrols also continued their search for refugees or captives.

Shortly after arriving at Camp Release, Sibley established a military commission, composed of five of his officers and an attorney from St. Paul. The commission was given the task of assigning culpability to those Indians identified as having perpetrated crimes during the uprising. The foundation for these charges was largely predicated on the testimony of women who had been held captive. Their accounts were collected by the Reverend Stephen Riggs, a missionary of twenty-five years' experience among the Minnesota Sioux.

Charges against the accused ranged from murder, to rape and robbery, to what was simply termed outrages against settlers and soldiers. Although a precedent for military commissions had been established by the army back in January 1862 for use in specific wartime situations, the

Young boy survivor identifying Indian participants in the uprising

Camp Lincoln

commission's use in adjudicating the guilt of Indians accused of criminal acts was a questionable interpretation of the army's ruling. Questionable or not, Sibley proceeded, and with General Pope's full acquiescence. Sibley charged the commission with the responsibility of ensuring that each Indian tried was accorded due process and the benefit of reasonable doubt. Notwithstanding, in many instances, convicting evidence was often circumstantial and testimony brief.

The commission heard testimony for some six weeks, by the end of which time it had determined the guilt of 303 Indians, for which the punishment was death. It had been Sibley's intention to hang all who were judged guilty, and, having General Pope's concurrence, he was prepared to proceed with the executions. However, neither officer had anticipated the need to execute 300 people, Indian or otherwise. Pope, accordingly, elected to refer the matter to the president, an option open to him under the articles of war. The list of those found guilty was telegraphed to Washington, where, on November 10, President Lincoln directed General Pope to provide com-

Two depictions of the mass hanging of thirty-eight Sioux Indians by the U.S. government at Mankato, Minnesota

plete trial records. The president wanted to distinguish between those Indians actually found guilty of criminal acts and those who had fought in the various battles of the uprising.

Meanwhile, the condemned Indians were moved downriver to a site named Camp Lincoln, near Mankato. The downriver journey to Camp Lincoln brought forth the wrath of the local populace, especially at New Ulm, where citizens attacked and wounded fifteen Indians and soldiers. When it was learned that an army of angry citizens planned to attack Camp Lincoln, the Indians were removed to a more secure structure in Mankato, there to await their fate.

On December 6, President Lincoln approved the death sentence for thirty-nine of those condemned. Later, one of the thirty-nine received a reprieve because his conviction was judged to have been based on weak testimony. The decision had not been an easy one for President Lincoln, who had been urged to show mercy and leniency by many easterners and the clergy, who noted how the deplorable system of Indian management had led to the uprising. "I felt it down to my boots," said Lincoln.[5] On the other hand, angry midwesterners, particularly Minnesotans, were not at all inclined to be merciful.

The date of execution had been set for December 19, but was then extended a week to allow time for additional preparations. Of those convicted, all but two accepted a Christian baptism and twenty-four were admitted into the Roman Catholic faith, thus providing some measure of satisfaction to those missionaries who had labored so long and hard among the Sioux.

At 10 A.M. on December 26, the thirty-eight condemned Santees mounted a scaffold and were there executed by hanging. The event was witnessed by 1,400 soldiers and a large crowd of civilian onlookers. It remains the largest public execution in U.S. history.

Teepees of Sioux Indians camped at Fort Snelling

Exile

The Sioux uprising of 1862 not only produced a bloodbath among the settlers of western Minnesota, its long-term effect on the Santee Sioux was far-reaching, resulting not only in the loss of their annuities, but also of their home territory along the Minnesota River. It is likely that this displacement would have occurred in the course of time anyway, but the uprising certainly hastened the process and did so in an atmosphere of anger and retribution that would not otherwise have been a part of such an uprooting.

Following the retrieval of the captives at Camp Release, all of the Indians who had not been found guilty—some 1,700—were transferred to Fort Snelling and confined there until a final disposition was decided upon. The decision to transfer these Indians to Fort Snelling was based on a concern that to leave them in the Minnesota River Valley was to invite harsh reprisal from enraged white settlers.

In spring of 1863, those 326 Santees still held as prisoners at Mankato were transferred to Camp McClellan, near Davenport, Iowa, where they remained for three years. Approximately 120 died in confinement, but the remainder were released in 1866 and allowed to rejoin families who had been relocated in Nebraska.

Meanwhile, the Sioux who had been held in confinement at Fort Snelling were shipped downriver to St. Louis in the spring of 1866 and relocated to reservations in eastern Dakota Territory. The relocation project, as it turned out, was all-encompassing and also included nearly 2,000 Winnebagos, who had been located in Blue Earth County, Minnesota, of which Mankato is the county seat. Although the Winnebagos had not been a part of the uprising, the public was scarcely in a mood to discriminate between good and bad Indians. The citizenry wanted all the Sioux and Winnebagos to be removed from Minnesota soil. As a consequence, by June 1863, the Winnebagos found themselves occupying a reservation in eastern Dakota, adjacent to their traditional enemies the Sioux. During the 1870s and 1880s, a few small groups of Sioux managed to return to Minnesota, but most would remain in Dakota Territory, the land of their exile.

Little Crow's wife and two children at Fort Snelling prison compound

General Alfred H. Sully

The Return and Death of Little Crow, July 3, 1863

Following the Battle of Wood Lake, Little Crow and perhaps 200 or so of his followers disappeared into the vastness of Dakota Territory, where his efforts to form an Indian alliance were as unsuccessful as they had been in Minnesota. A visit to Fort Garry (today's Winnipeg, Manitoba) also failed to elicit support either from Canadian authorities or from the Indians of that area.

Increasingly, Little Crow felt hostility and resistance no matter where he turned. In spring 1863, Little Crow, his son Wowinape, and a party of seventeen others made their way back to Minnesota. Perhaps, as his biographer, Gary Clayton Anderson, theorizes, the chief, believing that his days were numbered, desired to return the tribe's sacred medicine bundles to their traditional home.

In any case, by late June, Taoyateduta's party had reached the vicinity of the Yellow Medicine River. Shortly after reaching the area, some members of the party attacked and killed two members of the Amos Dustin family near Howard Lake, west of St. Paul. Whether Little Crow participated in the attack is not clear, although one of the victims, Mrs. Dustin, is said to have identified him before she died from her wounds.

Following the attack, the band separated, with some returning to Canada, others going south. Little Crow and Wowinape, however, chose to remain in the area around Hutchinson. On the evening of July 3, the pair was spotted while picking berries by a farmer named Nathan Lamson and his son Chauncey, who were out hunting. Undetected, the elder Lamson approached the two Indians, took aim, and fired. The bullet hit Little Crow in the leg, but the chief was able to return fire. Lamson's second shot struck Little Crow in the chest and proved fatal. He died shortly thereafter. After preparing his father's body for burial, Wowinape slipped away from the scene to find his mother's people in Dakota Territory.

Meanwhile, a frightened Chauncey Lamson, fearing that his father had been killed, skipped off during the exchange of shots and ran into Hutchinson to spread the story, which attracted more than a little attention owing to the recent incident at Howard Lake. Nathan Lamson had no idea as to the identity of the man he had killed, only that it had been an Indian. Little Crow's body was later taken to Hutchinson, where it was scalped and dismembered. Although the remains were believed to be those of Little Crow, positive identification could not be made until Wowinape related the story of his father's death to Sibley's soldiers when they captured him in August. A year later, Nathan Lamson was awarded a $500 bounty for killing the Santee leader. In the years following Little Crow's death, souvenir hunters claimed portions of his remains. In 1896, his skull and arm bones were presented to the Minnesota Historical Society, where they remained until 1971 when they were returned to his descendants.

Notes

1. *War of the Rebellion, Official Records*, Series I, Vol. XIII, pp. 278–279.
2. Ibid., p. 224.
3. Ibid., p. 248.
4. Oehler, *The Great Sioux Uprising*, p. 197.
5. Ibid., p. 213.

Epilogue

Although peace had largely returned to the Minnesota frontier by the autumn of 1862, concern about more Indian troubles in the future remained at the forefront of many minds, including those of Governor Alexander Ramsey and General John Pope. Indeed, scattered incidents during the next several months, such as the one at Howard Lake, kept the flame of concern burning brightly.

The aftermath of Wood Lake had witnessed a great Sioux diaspora from Minnesota. In addition to those convicted of criminal behavior and executed or imprisoned, and those relocated to Fort Snelling, a great many—perhaps as many as 5,000—exclusive of Little Crow's immediate followers, had fled to the vastness of Dakota Territory. The great majority of these were Upper Sioux people who had not been involved in the uprising, but feared punishment nevertheless and had accordingly moved beyond the reach of the white man's soldiers . . . or so they thought.

General Pope's concern was that these bands of Minnesota Santees would unite with their Siouan kinsmen, the Yanktons and Yanktonais, and perhaps even the Teton Lakota of the trans-Missouri region. As Pope saw it, the best way to address this potential threat was to follow up with a punitive strike. Accordingly, as summer 1863 approached, Pope prepared to send two columns into the field. One, under General Sibley, was to march northwestward from Fort Ridgely into the Devil's Lake region of east-central North Dakota. A second expedition, headed up by General Alfred Sully, was to strike out from Fort Randall, near the present border of South Dakota and Nebraska, and move north, up the Missouri River Valley. The idea here was to catch the Indians between the two forces. It was a strategy that was employed time and again in the Indian wars on the Great Plains, though seldom with the success envisioned at the outset.

Sibley commenced his campaign on June 16, 1863, with a ponderous column of more than 3,000 infantry, supported by 200 wagons. During the month of July, Sibley battled and defeated the Indians at Big Mound on the twenty-fourth, Dead Buffalo Lake on the twenty-sixth, and Stony Lake on the twenty-eighth. After waiting in vain to rendezvous with General Sully near present-day Bismarck, North Dakota, Sibley elected to terminate his campaign on August 1 and return to Minnesota.

Sully, meanwhile, delayed by low water in the Missouri, did not reach the Bismarck area until the end of August, where he discovered that Sibley had been there and left. However, learning of an Indian force in the area, Sully pursued and subsequently attacked and routed a large Indian village at Whitestone Hill, near present Ellendale, North Dakota, on September 3, 1863.

Although the battles fought by Sibley and Sully during the course of the 1863 campaign might themselves be viewed as victories, the real objective of the campaign—to break the back of the Santee bands that were still regarded as a threat—had not been realized. As a consequence, it was decided a second effort was needed.

June 1864 again found General Sully moving up the Missouri River Valley with two brigades consisting mostly of cavalry and some artillery, totaling 2,200 men. On July 28, Sully's expedition clashed with a force of 1,600 Lakotas, Yanktonais, and Santees at Tahchakuty Mountain—"The Place Where They Killed the Deer"–called Killdeer Mountain by the whites. The fight was a daylong affair observed by Indian noncombatants—with the Sioux finally giving way to Sully's superior numbers, supported by artillery. By dark the Indians had abandoned their village and moved off into the Badlands of the Little Missouri River. After destroying the village, Sully pursued the Indians into the Badlands, where skirmishes took place during the next few days before Sully finally elected to terminate the campaign on August 9.

Although fear of further Indian trouble haunted many Minnesotans after the 1862 uprising, the campaigns of 1863 and 1864 did much to quiet those fears. However, despite the victories at Whitestone Hill and Killdeer Mountain, the campaigns failed to bring about any real resolution to the Indian problem on the northern plains. Sibley and Sully had only managed to push the Indian frontier farther west, beyond the Missouri River, where it would take another fifteen years and several military campaigns to pacify the region.

Touring the Sites

Those wishing to explore the area will find easy access from any quarter. Travelers coming from the west on I-94 may exit the interstate at any one of several points, following state and U.S. highways to the central area of the uprising. A good starting point is Montevideo at the junction of U.S. 212 and state Highways 7 and 59. From the greater Minneapolis area, follow U.S. 212 to the uprising area. Travelers heading east or west along I-90 may exit the interstate at Blue Earth and follow U.S. 169 to Mankato.

The Forts of the Minnesota Uprising

Fort Snelling: Four main military posts were active in the region during the Minnesota uprising. The oldest of these, Fort Snelling, dated to 1819. Built on a high bluff at the junction of the Minnesota and Mississippi Rivers, its mission was to cover the far northwest frontier, protecting the trade interests of the fledgling United States. Originally called Cantonment New Hope and later Fort St. Anthony after the nearby Falls of St. Anthony, it was renamed Fort Snelling in honor of Colonel Josiah Snelling (1782–1828). As colonel of the Fifth U.S. Infantry, Snelling had been charged with the task of erecting three military posts on the northwest frontier, of which Fort Snelling was the most important.

The famous slave, Dred Scott, whose master was a physician at Fort Snelling during the 1830s, based his case for freedom on the argument that he had lived on free soil, an argument the United States Supreme Court subsequently rejected. Today, the site, located in Fort Snelling State Park at the junction of state Highways 5 and 55, is operated by the Minnesota Historical Society and contains some seventeen buildings, including a history center.

Fort Ripley: During the 1840s and 1850s, as a result of recent treaties with the Indians of the area, the U.S. Army reinforced its military presence in the region by erecting three additional forts in the Minnesota country. The first of these, Fort Ripley—originally named Fort Gaines—was located near the junction of the Crow Wing and Mississippi Rivers (south of Brainerd on Route 371).

Built in 1849, Fort Ripley had a mission to control the Sioux, Chippewa (Ojibway), and Winnebagos, whose perpetual warring and squabbling tended to disrupt the important fur trade.

The site of the original post may be found today some thirty miles west of Mille Lacs, although not much remains of the original structure, which was abandoned by the army in 1877. The old post is located on today's Camp Ripley Military Reservation (National Guard), and permission of the camp commander is required to visit the site.

Fort Ridgely: Located on a broad bench nearly two hundred feet above the valley of the Minnesota River, near the Lower Sioux Agency, Fort Ridgely was built in 1853–1855. Of all the Minnesota forts, Ridgely was destined to play the most important role in the 1862 uprising. As with Fort Ripley, its mission was to provide a military presence in the event of trouble with the Indians. The post was named for Captain Randolph Ridgely, who died in the Mexican War. Actually, there were three Ridgely brothers, Henderson, Randolph, and Thomas, and the fort may have been named for any one or all three men.

Following the treaties of 1851, Henry Hastings Sibley, then congressional representative for the Minnesota Territory, recommended that a military post be built in this area to keep an eye on the newly established Upper and Lower Sioux Reservations.

The resultant effort turned out to be a fort that was pretty to look at but poorly situated for defense, surrounded as it was by thickly timbered ravines on three of four sides. Fort Ridgely was under construction for two years. It was not built as a stockaded post, that is, not enclosed by log walls. When completed in 1855 it consisted of a group of buildings, two of which were constructed of native granite and fieldstone and the others of wood, arranged around a parade field.

In 1859, Fort Ridgely was selected to be a field artillery school, a decision that was to have a significant impact on the events of August 1862. The fort's garrison changed frequently, particularly following the outbreak of the Civil War, when regular army units were transferred east to serve against the Confederacy. In April 1862, Companies B and C of the Fifth Minnesota Infantry arrived at the fort, with Company C slated to move on to take up station at Fort Ripley on the upper reaches of the Mississippi River. It was these units that were to bear the brunt of the Sioux attacks during the early days of the uprising.

Following the uprising and the subsequent removal of Indians from southern Minnesota, a new influx of settlers poured into the state. With the Indian threat now largely nonexistent, Fort Ridgely's presence in the area was no longer required and, in 1867, the garrison was withdrawn. Settlers gradually tore down those buildings that were still standing. In 1880, the site was opened to settlement and in 1911, the Minnesota legislature established Fort Ridgely State Park, which today may be visited just west of Route 4, some four miles south of Fairfax. Some archaeological and restoration work has been done and the state operates a museum and visitor center.

Fort Abercrombie: The fourth fort in the region, Fort Abercrombie was technically not located in Minnesota, but rather on the west side of the Red River, just across the line in present North Dakota. Built in 1858, Fort Abercrombie was the first permanent military post to be built in Dakota Territory. In addition to monitoring Indian activities, Abercrombie had as its mission protecting travelers bound for Canada and overland, across Dakota. The site is located near the present town of Abercrombie, forty-five miles south of Fargo. Take I-29 to Exit 37, then east to Abercrombie.

Recommended Reading

Anderson, Gary Clayton, and Alan R. Woolworth. *Through Dakota Eyes: Narrative Accounts of the Minnesota Indian War of 1862*. St. Paul: Minnesota Historical Society Press, 1988

———. *Little Crow: Spokesman for the Sioux*. St. Paul: Minnesota Historical Society Press, 1986

Beck, Paul N. *Soldier, Settler, and Sioux: Fort Ridgely and the Minnesota River Valley 1853–1857.* Sioux Falls, SD: Augustana College, 2000

Carley, Kenneth. *The Sioux Uprising of 1862*. St. Paul: Minnesota Historical Society, 1976

Clodfelter, Micheal. *The Dakota War: The United States Army Versus the Sioux, 1862–1865*. Jefferson, NC: McFarland & Company, Inc.

Cozzens, Peter. *General John Pope: A Life for the Nation*. Urbana and Chicago: University of Illinois Press, 2000

Folwell, William Watts. *A History of Minnesota*, Vol. II. St. Paul: Minnesota Historical Society, 1924

Jones, Robert Huhn. *The Civil War in the Northwest: Nebraska, Wisconsin, Iowa, Minnesota, and the Dakotas*. Norman: University of Oklahoma Press, 1960

Oehler, C. M. *The Great Sioux Uprising*. New York: Oxford University Press, 1959

Schultz, Duane. *Over the Earth I Come: The Great Sioux Uprising of 1862*. New York: St. Martin's Press, 1992

Index